THE APPARITIONS OF
THE BLESSED VIRGIN MARY TODAY

GW00771117

The Apparitions
of the
Blessed Virgin Mary
Today

René Laurentin

VERITAS

Published 1990 by
Veritas Publications
7-8 Lower Abbey Street
Dublin 1

Original French language edition of
Multiplication des apparitions de la Vierge aujourd'hui
published and copyright 1988 by
Librairie Arthème Fayard
75 rue des Saint-Pères
75278 Paris cedex 06
France

ISBN 1 85390 054 0

Translated by Luke Griffin
Cover design by Banahan McManus, Dublin
Typesetting by Printset & Design Ltd, Dublin
Printed in the Republic of Ireland by The Leinster Leader Ltd.

CONTENTS

PART I

Judging apparitions

1

A COMPLEX PROBLEM

Apparitions of the Virgin are on the increase. But is it really the Virgin? And what does she want to say to us? Many people wonder about these questions, genuinely seeking a response. Others simply claim that the question does not exist for they already know the answer: 'This proliferation of apparitions is a psycho-sociological phenomenon and is no doubt pathological. The wisest thing is to ignore the phenomenon, put it to one side, as indeed the Church has done. There has been no official recognition of any apparition that took place over the past fifty years or more.'

Why worry about apparitions?
With a shrug of the shoulders people will no doubt say: 'There goes Laurentin on his apparition trail. Has he been completely taken in? What is he doing getting himself into that mess?' I asked a colleague whose culture, science and spiritual insight has made of him a most eminent mariologist, if he had been to Medjugorje. 'No', he replied wisely, 'and that is how I retain my reputation.'

These incidents and others are evidence of the extent to which apparitions have become a source of contradiction and uneasiness. 'When the Blessed Virgin appears the family circle does not go wild with joy.' The clergy, true to its tradition, does not welcome an apparition as good tidings. They see it as a rather unsavoury event. It has always been so. From Lourdes to Île Bouchard, parish priests have never allowed themselves to be convinced in a hurry. The first reaction of those in charge, no doubt a legitimate reaction, is to look for the flaw, and to cover up, suppress or limit the impact of the unusual phenomenon. In many instances an end is put to the entire affair right from the start by a sharp and forceful intervention, often facilitated by the obedient compliance of the visionaries. Thus the majority of apparitions disappear before they are even talked about.

The reaction to miracles is similar. Igor Barrère presented a television programme on 4 April 1988 on TF1, in the course of which Jeanne Frétel, whose cure at Lourdes had been officially recognised, admitted that her experience led to rejection by her Catholic neighbours.

I emphasise these negative attitudes not because they surprise or upset me, but because the unease they express underlines the real question we must face, at the risk of falling for an illusion (cf. Appendix 2, pp. 139-143).

The need for some introductory remarks is becoming apparent. A simple recital of the apparitions could give rise to misunderstanding. This in turn could lead to hasty rejection on the one hand, or to over-enthusiastic acceptance on the other. The whole question of apparitions is more complex and delicate than appears at first sight. We have to learn the correct approach to the subject.

So, what have I been doing in this quagmire? It was not I who chose the apparitions; rather it was the apparitions themselves that enlisted my services.

I had no personal inclination to get into that particular field. By the time I had finished my two doctoral theses on theology and literature I had not yet been to Lourdes, even though one of my uncles was deeply involved. It was Mgr Theas who unwittingly involved me. In 1953 he asked me to prepare a 'Theology of Lourdes' for the International Marian Congress in Rome in 1954. I had the impression that the task would not be too much of a burden; after all, the history of the apparitions was well-established and all that would be required was a rapid reflection on it. I was soon to discover that a proper history had still to be done. Over half the documents, particularly the early ones, were undiscovered. Authors were not in agreement over the number of apparitions: most suggested eighteen, while Cros and Trochu, reputed to be the most reliable, said nineteen. They were wrong. A proper text of the words of Our Lady spoken in local dialect had not been established. The essential requirements of truth eventually led me to publish over thirty volumes: *Documents, Histoire des Apparitions; Vie, Paroles, Visage de Bernadette,* etc. If I was to be taken seriously nothing less would do. Being scientific means being exhaustive and verifiable. The words spoken by Our Lady at Lourdes were said in the context of a very complex historical situation and an understanding of her message required an unimpeachable appreciation of that situation. The precision of this work had the advantage of putting an end to the incessant attacks on Lourdes from the *Libre Pensée* and from Dr Valot. The polemic was nourished by what people appeared to want to hide.

I opened up everything, even things that were inadmissible and in that general context everything made sense, even Bernadette's so-called retraction, resulting as it did from a trick by the police commissioner, Jacomet, which I discovered and clarified. The main advantage of this work was the filtering out of impurities and the clarification of the meaning of Lourdes, thus freeing it from local prejudices and political bias and recentering it on the gospel, the message of which is re-echoed in Our Lady's message. Thus, this work provided a method and a model for a serious study of apparitions, a study which had been neglected by theologians and left to wallow in the domain of half-truths associated with popular fervour. I was therefore invited to write the history and investigate the theology associated with other sanctuaries. The requests were numerous and some had to be refused. (In the case of Fatima it was with some regret, because of sheer lack of time, though my role as consultant did afford me great pleasure.)

The Bishop of Laval, Mgr Guilhem, commissioned a similar study on Pontmain to mark the centenary of the apparitions in 1971. I spent five years working on the four volumes which were published. At some risk I unearthed the carefully concealed retraction of one of the visionaries, Jeanne-Marie Lebossé. This resulted in a reprimand from Cardinal Richaud. A careful study of the retraction made it abundantly clear that Jeanne-Marie Lebossé, a fearless and authentic visionary, and one who was maltreated on that account, had become the victim of a profound attack of scrupulousness. And I had rehabilitated her. To my surprise the local bishop regretted this. Cardinal Richaud died before the rehabilitation, which I hadn't expected to uncover, was published; had he seen it he might well have pardoned me.

The Lazarist Fathers and Jean Guitton requested a study on the miraculous medal and Catherine Labouré for the centenary of her death and the fiftieth anniversary of the apparitions. This work took nine years (1972-80) and resulted in six volumes. Again, I exhumed the memoirs of Father Coste, a Lazarist. These memoirs were deemed fatal to the cause of Catherine Labouré and her apparitions, yet a careful study revealed that they were harmless, based as they were on unrelenting prejudice against miracles.

For many years I kept aloof from apparitions that were currently happening. In the first instance because they were generally deemed suspect and priests were frequently forbidden to attend. I have always obeyed the Church. I still do, even today, when bishops forbid me to lecture about apparitions in their dioceses. But there are other bishops who invite me and, indeed, chair my lectures. To become involved in current apparitions would be a risky business. But with increasing frequency I was invited to visit places of apparition.

Thus I eventually went to Medjugorje (Yugoslavia) after eighteen months of preliminary enquiries among a number of Croatians. I was encouraged by the fact that, initially, the local bishop was in favour of the apparitions. After my arrival I discovered, somewhat belatedly, that he had changed his views and was implacably opposed to the apparitions. He gave me his reasons. They were not sufficient to dissuade me from undertaking a study. Direct contact with the ecstatic visionaries, whom the bishop had not met, was a revelation for me. My previous contact with apparitions had been as a historian. I was working in the dark, restricted to interpreting the evidence of dusty archives and always regretting not having seen or spoken to Bernadette or Catherine Labouré. However conscientiously I wrote about Bernadette's ecstasy, it was at one remove. Now at first hand I was able to understand how and why no one could hear her voice when she spoke to Our Lady. I also had the extraordinary opportunity of submitting the visionaries to medical and scientific experiments. I realised to what extent a historian is a mere excavator of events buried in the past. I felt like an Egyptologist who, on visiting the Great Pyramid, had come face to face with Cheops and Nefertiti.

This surprise was followed by yet another. My first book on Medjugorje, which I had put together in haste, was an extraordinary success. There were several reprints of 10,000 copies each, and each reprint sold out within a week. The subsequent edition, which came out a month later, was eagerly awaited. But above all, this book provoked a huge correspondence which was in itself a sign for me. Many readers had changed their lives for the better. For the first time in my life many people wrote to me: 'Your book has converted me.' This was indeed a surprise. I was taken aback. I drew the logical conclusion: for once I had not worked in vain. At a time when the garden of the Church is indeed barren should one not concentrate on an area that bore such an abundance of good fruit? All the more so as these apparitions were threatened from two different quarters: the Church and the state. The communist government had to be against them in principle. The bishop, who is an ardent advocate of Lourdes and was at one time favourably disposed towards the apparitions, had become a strong adversary for strange reasons that had to do with local conflicts.

In a broader context, given that scepticism towards apparitions had become second nature to the Church, the Catholic press gave very unfavourable coverage to the apparitions at Medjugorje. The extreme right viewed it as diabolical mimicry of Fatima; the centre left, which is well-represented in the media, amplified and exaggerated the denunciations and false accusations emanating from the bishop's palace at Mostar. They even added some of their own.

The apparitions have brought about many conversions and have given rise to a spiritual movement comparable to that which surrounded St Francis of Assisi. The genuineness of the apparitions required emergency assistance, because the conditions of repression and lack of equilibrium that surrounded the pilgrimages were such as to lead one to suspect that they would deviate from the straight and narrow, along the road of rebellion or depression, bitterness or illuminism.

I had a written invitation from Mgr Gahamany to visit Kibeho in Rwanda. Again I was edified both by the visionaries and by the fruit of their actions. I grappled with the factors which, in spite of the bishop's favourable attitude, are hindering the recognition of these apparitions and the accompanying pastoral work.

Are there too many apparitions?
On this question a new element comes into play. Paradoxically, at a time when certain visionaries believed their apparitions to be the last of all time, lo and behold, apparitions seem to be on the increase. I have endeavoured to investigate the reasons for such a disturbing proliferation. Was it perhaps an epidemic of the variety so rigorously put down by Cardinal Ottaviani during the years following the Second World War? How is this resurgence to be explained?

1.   Perhaps it is a transitory phenomenon of our complex times? Necromancers, clairvoyants, fortune tellers and alternative medicines are enjoying unprecedented popularity. Add to this the spiritual techniques associated with oriental religions. Perhaps the increasing number of apparitions ought to be seen as part of this spontaneous wave and, thus, deserving of caution and prudence.

Moreover the arms race, 'the balance of fear', creates an apocalyptic climate. Humanity is expectant, on the look-out for signs, open to the symbolic projections of its own subjectivity. Troubled times provide a climate favourable to apparitions. Finally, there are those who placed all their hopes on the apparently unlimited possibilities of the scientific approach. They are beginning to understand that science does not resolve and will never resolve all the problems of life. They look elsewhere. Hence there is a religious revival which, alas, is not the result of a revival of faith. Our times are marked by a new curiosity about religion without a sufficient basis in faith.

These explanations, based on human subjectivity, are not without foundation. Without the receptivity of a subject there would be no apparitions, but, as a corollary, subjectivity can lead to illusory apparitions.

2.   There is nothing a priori to exclude us from looking for an explanation in the realms of objective reality. The Blessed Virgin's mission is that of a mother to our world. According to Grignon de Montfort, this mission will be intensified in the last days. Does not the increase in apparitions correspond to a certain urgency; perhaps not the end of the world, but at least a serious historical turning-point at the threshold of the third millennium?

Because of invitations I had received I was able to investigate a number of different locations where apparitions took place. The general aim was somehow to expose this very proliferation. But more often than expected, my investigations yielded positive results. The apparitions which took place in Argentina (San Nicolas), Mexico, Rwanda (Kibeho), Syria (Damascus), Italy (Schio) and Korea (Naju) etc. offered no evidence of anything pathological. Though some of my investigations did provide evidence of deviations and illusory apparitions, the majority of them did not merit consignment to that scrap heap reserved for apparitions which seem to be suspect even in the most minor way.

This is based on the adage *bonum ex quacumque causa, malum ex quocumque defectu* (a thing is good when all of it is good, bad if there is the slightest defect). If this yardstick were to be used Lourdes would never have been recognised — Lourdes, where Bernadette's apparitions (which could have been suspect because of her asthmatic condition) were followed by a veritable epidemic of visionaries that at one time numbered more than fifty.

An authorised question

While these matters were running through my mind, Cardinal Sin, Archbishop of Manila, put me to the test. At the end of a congress on the theme of consecration he invited me to give a lecture: 'Current apparitions of Mary — what does she want to say?'

This is a very difficult question. To answer it might appear the height of imprudence, an anticipation, almost a usurpation, of the official judgement of the Church. Reflecting on the answer I had received from my eminent colleague in Rome, I began to think that a theologian could not tackle this question without tarnishing his reputation. The title reduced my subject matter to the apparitions of the Blessed Virgin; too narrow a focus, it might be said. Why did I finally accept?

First of all, every genuine question merits an answer. As a matter of principle I do not refuse to face up to questions that appear troublesome. This question was asked by a cardinal from the Third World, a shining light in the Church for his contribution to spirituality, catechesis and the practical effects of consecration, a leading Roman diplomat, prominent in the difficult dialogue with Marxism both in the USSR and on mainland China.

In addition, his question was real. It was a question being asked not only by his priests, but by many others, a question born of unease and one which no one yet had tackled.

Urgency or prudence?

Firstly, there is a serious dilemma: should one show haste or prudence? Those who were drawn to the apparitions and who were converted have, on returning home, been met with: 'You shouldn't go there. As long as the Church has not recognised them we should wait'. If they *had* waited they would not have been converted. Also, the grace which they have received seems to abound in those places where they received it. And again Our Lady's messages to visionaries seem to have a strong note of urgency: The world is in danger; Pray and do penance...

So then, prudence or haste? Most ecclesiastical advisers seem to favour prudence, while Our Lady seems to insist on the urgency of the matter. For many Christians this really is a dilemma.

But in fact it may well prove to be a false dilemma which cries out for a viable solution: haste and prudence in our urgency. We can pray, fast and be converted speedily according to the messages which echo the gospel, while prudently awaiting the judgment of the Church.

This misunderstanding and the apparent contradictions are symptomatic of the confusion which reigns. Our next chapter will clarify this confused situation by tackling the question: Why are apparitions a sign of contradiction? Why are they so low down in the Church's priorities? Is there a reason for this? Or, again, to what degree are apparitions ignored on the one hand and exaggerated on the other? How do we transcend this contradiction and get on with complying with these requests from heaven when they are authentic, and at the same time, avoid the illusions of the devil or of subjectivity?

2

THE PARADOX OF APPARITIONS IN THE CHURCH—WHAT IS THE OUTCOME?

What is the value and the function of apparitions in the Church? This is the basic question which must be addressed if we are to come to grips with all the other questions. Polemics and passion are useless; the rules surrounding apparitions are simple and paradoxical; there are numerous pitfalls and many traps to be avoided.

The supernatural as visible, a low priority

It is a fact, at least in modern times, that apparitions are placed at the bottom of the Church's received values. Theology is nervous of the supernatural made visible. Is it not a contradiction of the very nature of our faith which is 'the assurance of things hoped for, the conviction of things not seen' *(Heb 11:1)*? The words of Christ to doubting Thomas seem to confirm this: 'Blessed are those who have not seen and yet believe' *(Jn 20:29)*.

Biblical theology presents this revelation as the Word of God. Other revelations which do not enjoy this status are seen as intrusive, with a tendency to overestimate their own authority. Dogmatic theology defines 'private revelations' in a negative fashion, almost as accretions which enjoy no authority.

Fundamental theology also confines private revelations to the bottom of the list. Melchior Cano did not even list them among his ten theological sources:

> Private revelations are of no concern to the Catholic faith and do not belong to the principle or foundation of ecclesiastical doctrine, which is genuine and authentic theology, because faith is not a private virtue but rather a community virtue (in *Opera, De locis theologicis,* XII, 3, conclusion 3, Éditions Vassairi 1746, p. 350).

Moral theology generally avoids this whole ambiguous area though it might well find a place for it in the treatise on prophecy. Mystical theology shows a marked reserve towards these dangerous epiphenomena, to which no importance ought to be attached:

> The soul that is pure and simple, prudent and humble, will use all its powers of strength and diligence to reject these revelations and visions as the most dangerous of temptations (Saint John of the Cross, *Montée du Carmel*, 2, 27; Oeuvres spirituelles, Paris, Seuil, 1929, p. 276).

Church history treats this whole domain as a poor relation. Canon law touches only on the precautions to be taken in order to limit or suppress these phenomena.

All these precautions derive from a very understandable perception of the risks involved when the supernatural is made visible in an extraordinary way: illuminism and deviations. Moreover this caution also derives from the necessity of clearly understanding that revelation ends with the death of the last apostle, the last of the witnesses chosen by Christ. A new revelation can therefore add nothing to the revelation of Christ as such. Indeed if a revelation alleged that it added something, Paul's statement would apply: 'But even if we, or an angel from heaven, should preach to you a gospel contrary to that which we preached to you, let him be accursed' *(Gal 1:8)*.

It is perfectly correct to contrast the absolute certitude of the revelation, infallibly guaranteed by the Church, with the relative incertitude of apparitions, even where they are officially recognised, because this very recognition is only an indicator of their probability. The infallibility of the Church comes into play only in respect of the Credo. Infallibility is not involved in that laborious process of discernment which surrounds an apparition: Is it really Christ or the Virgin who is appearing? Perhaps it is just a pious illusion? Does not the case of visionaries call for extreme prudence?

The conclusion reached by many that apparitions are a minor and indeed dangerous phenomenon, is not without foundation. It is better to err on the side of caution than on the side of enthusiasm. In any case this is what has inspired the Church's cautious attitude since the mid-1920s to such an extent that no apparition since Beauraing (1932) and Banneux (1933) had been officially recognised by the Catholic Church until the most recent exception of Finca Betania (1987). We will examine this case later on (see pp.00). An understanding of the function of miracles is necessary if we are to proceed beyond this impasse.

The function of apparitions

Their function is not to complete the gospel in which Christ revealed all that is necessary for our salvation. Rather their function is to recall, to remove the scales from our eyes, to reopen our ears, to actualise the gospel, to insert it into our times and show, once more, its power to underline its own life-giving values. Thomas Aquinas held that apparitions have more to do with hope than with faith. They shape the future. They bring the gospel to life in a prophetic manner in new historic or geographic situations. These tangible signs, in proclaiming the immediacy, the presence, the familiarity and the power of the gospel, bring these gospel powers to life.

Apparitions therefore have an important role to play. When we understand their role we ought to welcome them joyfully as God's grace, a light guiding us through the night of faith. If God is disappointed by our indifference and decides to send his Son or Our Lady to repeat, with signs of fire and light, that which we have forgotten, to convert us, to involve us prophetically in the history of salvation, this is indeed Good News, urgent news, marking a turning point for the world.

Why, then, is there so much distrust, aggression and repression? History, based on solid precedents, will answer this question.

A noble lineage

The first item of importance is the noble lineage of apparitions which have an important place in the Bible from Abraham to Moses and the prophets.

Nor is their role diminished in the New Testament. Mary and Joseph enjoyed visions and private revelations before the birth of Christ. Christ himself was no stranger to visions: the tempter at the outset of his ministry; Moses and Elijah at the transfiguration; a consoling angel at the hour of his agony. The apparitions of the risen Christ became the cornerstone of the faith of the apostles and of the Church. Not discounting the importance of the phrase: 'Blessed are those who have not seen but yet believe', both Peter and Paul were given the grace of radically important visions at the beginning of the history of the Church. Paul's conversion was due to a vision of the risen Christ (Acts 9) and it was in a vision that Peter was invited to open up membership of the Church, hitherto strictly confined to Jews, to all, even pagans (Acts 10) — and these are just two of the visions outlined in the Acts of the Apostles.

It is true that the demythologisers reduce all this area to 'manageable proportions', even to subjectivity. But this is to impoverish revelation itself, to stunt and amputate it beyond recognition, in the name of ideologies that are foreign to the notion of revelation.

Apparitions and private revelations did not come to an end with apostolic times. The entire history of the Church bears witness to them, right down to more recent times when the very proliferation of apparitions, though a cause of astonishment, is nevertheless a response to a basic need and an enduring function, however modest that function may be.

Attention to prudence and discernment

The Bible warns against false visions and false prophets and calls for prudence and discernment. It invites us to beware of the danger of illuminism and uncontrolled imagination. The Old Testament oscillates between outright condemnation of false prophets and visions on the one hand and, on the other, laments that there are 'no more prophets and no longer any visions in Israel'.[1] The prophets announced the feast of Pentecost as the happy reappearance of these gifts: 'And it shall come to pass afterward, and I will pour out my spirit on all flesh; your sons and your daughters shall prophesy, your old men shall dream dreams, and your young men shall see visions. Even upon the menservants and maidservants in those days I will pour out my spirit' *(Jl 2:28-29)*. Peter celebrates the fulfilment of this prophecy during Pentecost (Act 2:17). Thus, while we should welcome apparitions, our welcome should be tempered with caution and an effort at verification and control. We ought to avoid any imbalance between openness and receptivity and that modest prudence which prevents us from straying.

Which historical factors have devalued apparitions?

For a long time in the life of the Church apparitions were well-received, but due to their very ambiguity, historical circumstances and other factors have gradually eroded this acceptance.

1. Montanism — a prestigious charismatic movement that had its origins in the second century. The popularity of the movement tended to undermine the authority of the bishops. It eventually ended in schism and illuminism. One still wonders at the degree of orthodoxy which was maintained to the extent that the movement numbered among its ranks Tertullian, still honoured as a Father of the Church, in spite of his lapse into heresy at the end of his days. This movement represented a traumatic rupture in the Church of the second and third centuries. As a result, the initial welcome gave way to distrust and suppression. A visionary, even an authentic one, who did not give immediate proof of obedience and humility, ran a very serious risk: *Corruptio optimi pessima* — corruption of the best gives rise to the worst (situation).

2. Institutional authority feels itself under attack by apparitions. According to a study by Karl Rahner, this is a factor which goes against them: 'The history of mystical theology is a history of the devaluation, at least in a speculative fashion, of prophetism and a promotion of pure, infused, non-prophetic contemplation ... and because the former is more dangerous than the latter, it runs a greater risk of being in conflict with the permanent official organisms of the Church' (*Les révélations privées,* in *Revue d'ascétique et mystique* 25, 1949, p. 507).

The visionary who claims to have a direct line to heaven is often given more credence than a bishop or even the Pope himself. The gravity of the situation is often compounded by lack of clarity on the part of the authorities. Such was the case in the Middle Ages, when the suppression of charismatic groups and their associated apparitions was vigorously pursued by a feudal episcopate. What might have been productively and harmoniously harnessed, degenerated into unedifying conflict. Visionaries and prophets criticised the authorities, whose faith and morals were often not beyond reproach, and the authorities in turn condemned the insolence of the visionaries. Tension mounted, visionaries and charismatics lapsed into schism or were forced into drudgery. A case in point was the prophetic Dominican, Savonarola (1452-98).

Vatican II defused this tension. It reminded the Church that authority is service, that prophetic gifts and, indeed, the Holy Spirit, were given to the whole Church. Thus, American bishops were able to welcome the charismatic renewal movement even though it had its origins in the non-Catholic spirituality of pentecostalism. This was a blessing for the whole Church and for ecumenism. The prophetic openness of John Paul II is a continuation of this grace.

3.   At times of difficulty for the Church apparitions seem to spread uncontrollably. The increasing power of the communications media and the often inaccurate reporting of events of this nature tend to exacerbate problems for the authorities. The Fifth Lateran Council and the Council of Trent both issued edicts to encourage bishops to take a more critical and restrictive stance in these matters:

> We wish that ... such revelations should henceforth be reserved for examination by the Apostolic See before being made public or preached to the people. If this were to involve a risk of delays, or should some other circumstance dictate a different procedure, then the local Ordinary ought to be informed.... The latter, with the advice of three or four learned men, will subject the matter to diligent scrutiny. If, in their view, all things seem proper, and let this be for them a serious matter of conscience, then permission may be granted (Fifth Lateran Council, Session 11, 19 December 1516, in *Conciliorum O Ecumenicorum Decreta,* Bologna, Herder, 1962, p. 637).

At least the Council reminds us that we should 'not quench the Spirit' *(1 Thess 5:19),* but rather test and discern the spirits, because a whole body of Christian tradition continues to view apparitions as a sign of holiness and God's familiarity with humankind.

4.   The proliferation of apparitions which followed Beauraing (1932) and Banneux (1933) in Belgium, continued during and after the war. This is often the pattern in troubled times. Cardinal Ottaviani decided on a policy of strict repression. He stopped the canonisation of important mystics, such as Sister Faustina and Sister Yvonne-Aimée Malestroit, whose case I received permission to study and publish.[2] Sister Faustina's cause has been reopened, thanks to the intervention of John Paul II. Those were difficult times for Padre Pio and for others. Apart from the more

discreet repressive intervention which emanated from the secrecy of the Holy Office, Cardinal Ottaviani went public in a quite forthright article in *L'Osservatore Romano*. The article began with a quotation from Dante: 'Siate Cristiani, a muoveri più gravi!' ('Christians, do not allow yourselves to be moved in haste!') (A. Ottaviani, *L'Osservatore Romano*, 4 February 1951, no. 28).

This institutional repression, pursued by a man of strict traditional dogmatic persuasion, coincided, paradoxically, with a more radical progressive argument against apparitions. The reasons behind this argument were based on demythologisation and reductionism, tactics which were applied to the Easter appearances of the risen Christ and to the belief in the resurrection of the body. This reductionist movement brought a number of arguments to bear against apparitions:

1.   Rationalism did not allow for any contact between heaven and earth. God could not miraculously intervene in a given place. Scientism declared the miracle to be impossible and, as a consequence, apparitions to be mere hallucinations.

2.   At a deeper and more radical level the philosophy of idealism, which has dominated our era since Kant and Hegel, reduced to subjectivity, not only apparitions and other communications with the transcendent, but also all miracles and the resurrection of Christ himself. This philosophical system, according to which all that is known is knowledge, eliminated the dynamic tension between knowledge and reality and thereby allowed full sway to subjectivity in all things, but particularly in respect of apparitions. Freud's psychoanalysis, based as it was on the same philosophical tenets, was grist to the mill, offering an explanation of religious phenomena in general and of apparitions in particular, based on the drives of the libido and their sublimation, etc. The influence of psychoanalysis has permeated some Church circles and, as a result, some ecclesiastics have been led systematically to interpret apparitions as a product of subjectivity: 'When a visionary such as Bernadette sees the Virgin and those others who are present do not, I call this phenomenon, medically and scientifically, an hallucination.' This is the view of Oraison, who is clearly oblivious of the possible explanation based on an objective knowledge of the other world with the help of grace.

3.   To this we should add (at least at the level of methodology) the impact of scientific criticism, a central theme in our modern times. Scientific criticism, meaning a critical attitude, is of course a fundamental and necessary cultural value. We inherited the word and the attitude from the ancient Greeks. However, for them the root *crisis* simply meant judgement, control, careful verification. In our modern times it has come to mean suspicion and systematic doubt. Its proponents like to dwell on the example of Galileo: It is the earth which turns around the sun and not the sun around the earth. The truth is contrary to common sense. Scientific criticism has systematically attacked all transcendent truth, all divine intervention in our world: Mary's virginity, miracles, the Resurrection. The masters of suspicion gloried in this criticism of supreme values based so brilliantly on earthly values. The first among these was Marx who denied the existence of God and of the spiritual. Nietzsche knocked Christianity in favour of the essential value of the will for power. Freud, the demystifier of moral and religious values, which he treated as the cause of repression and neuroses, argued in favour of the basic drives of the libido which, once liberated, would bring us to proper self-knowledge and to health.

These are, in outline, the arguments through which scientific criticism endeavoured to reduce 'the things that are above' to mere earthly values, as if scientific criticism was the golden rule of science and the unique way to certitude.[3]

This is a strange illusion. True science acknowledges that doubt leads only to further doubt. Science does have rigorous controls, but these belong only to its second phase, that of verification. The first phase of science, the creative phase, is marked by an openness to reality that permits the positing of daring hypotheses, which at times seem to defy common sense. Sometimes these unlikely hypotheses win over the scepticism of so-called wiser beings.

The science of mechanics has progressed from paradox to paradox. The apparently absurd hypothesis on the origin of the continents was confirmed in spite of all expectations to the contrary. In the realms of science bold intuition is the spearhead of progress and the inevitable criticism belongs only to the second phase, involving careful and patient verification.

This method, which is so central to science, has often been neglected when matters of faith are under discussion. The cultivation of doubt and suspicion, as if this were the *ne plus ultra* of scientific method, was elevated to the status of virtue. Faith itself was thus undermined. As a gift of God, faith is robust, but this gift is rooted in human frailty. In theology, as in other sciences, doubt leads only to further doubts and, ultimately, to nothingness.

Again, as in the other sciences, theology is moved forward by bold and sometimes apparently risky hypotheses. The intuitive and prophetic function plays a central role. Faith and charity are the wellsprings of that action which, in the original sense of the word, edify both the Church and the believer. It is God acting on humankind through the inspiration of the Spirit. More often than not, faith offers its own proofs according to the gospel adage: 'He who does what is true comes to the light' *(Jn 3:21)*. Frequently apparitions 'do what is true' among the faithful, who return to prayer and to charity and bond themselves into living communities. At San Nicolas in Argentina, at Medjugorje in Yugoslavia, at Schio in Italy, communities are springing up with a new internal vitality.

It took communism to remind certain theologians that Christianity is a 'praxis', i.e. a theory, rooted in reality, which builds up the individual, structures society and shapes the future. Unfortunately many have forgotten that this 'praxis' is based, not on class struggle and hatred, but on charity, which promotes order and justice.

All the factors mentioned have contributed to the current devaluation of apparitions and to the repressive attitude with which they are greeted. Numerous 'expert committees' of psychologists, theologians and others have been set up by people allergic to positive discernment. Unusual events are judged from the outside, sifted through the mesh of their critical ideologies devoid of that sympathy which is necessary for an understanding, not only of religious facts, but of all poetry and music. Their assumptions and their extraordinary criteria would seem to require God to provide us with absolute proof. Christ himself formally refused to give such proof to the Pharisees (Mt 12:39). These 'experts' merely dig up scraps of evidence, which they conscientiously scrutinise in their studies.

Finally, the prophetic sense and the sense of discernment have diminished in the Church. Spiritual directors who should be the leaders in the field have often given way to psychologists and psychoanalysts who are (wrongly!) deemed to provide the same service in a more modern package. Their techniques often take no cognisance of the action of God. Spiritual direction and discernment have lost ground in the Church. This is certainly to the detriment of apparitions.

A malaise to be overcome
The devaluation of apparitions reached its zenith in the years 1950-80. All excesses provoke a reaction in the opposite direction. Though apparitions have a modest function within the Church, it is a real one and one which is necessary in certain circumstances. Thus once again we find that apparitions are flourishing.

But those who see their value and accept them are faced with no small difficulty. When a person who has been converted to Medjugorje finds himself being told by a priest that 'you are living in an illusion, yours is an attitude of disobedience because these apparitions have not been recognised...', he can only remain troubled and perplexed: 'I did not believe; now if (according to the Church) these apparitions which restored my faith are an illusion, should I not conclude, in all logic, that everything is an illusion, or perhaps I should look for religious truth outside the Church?' This is indeed a thorny problem of conscience.

This very problem is one of the reasons for my interest in apparitions. For many years I had noticed that individual pilgrims and, indeed, groups of pilgrims, were like sheep without a shepherd, whose only experience of the Church had been incomprehensible conflict. Left to themselves these devotees of apparitions risked becoming a 'church of apparitions', an odd collection of disparate groups. Sometimes these sheep without a shepherd were comforted by certain marginal priests, who seem to harbour bitterness against the official Church while favouring certain forms of illuminism.

Such was the case at San Damiano. Mama Rosa was certainly a holy woman. Her love of the Church, like her obedience to it, was unconditional. These virtues she shared with her two sisters, both nuns, one in Asia and the other in America. Both sisters were forbidden to visit her. Mama Rosa's first two children had been difficult births, both by caesarian section. When the third baby was on the way medical advice was adamant: 'Don't keep this child, it will be the death of you'. (Abortion was practised long before it was legal.)

She decided to continue her pregnancy. To the surprise of the doctors a baby girl was born, again by caesarian section. Both were alive, but the mother contracted puerperal fever, which confined her to hospital for several months. It was during this period that she had her apparitions.

How could it be said that there was no evidence of the supernatural? During her whole life she had counted on the supernatural, placing her trust in God alone. Objective inquiries discovered dozens, even hundreds, of cures that convinced doctors from many countries; many conversions and vocations were traced to this pilgrimage. If there is no evidence of the supernatural here, as had been so confidently declared, what signs of the supernatural are there in the rest of the Church? Systematic criticism of apparitions quenches the spirit which should be discerned; it sterilises what needs to be nursed with prudence and charity.

This pilgrimage has met with repression and opposition on the part of officials. It has been championed by certain marginal priests, particularly of the right wing traditionalist variety. The message of San Damiano has suffered accordingly, precisely because of the absence of normal pastoral care. A message from one of these protagonists confidently declares that communion in the hand is a sacrilege (12 March 1969). An 'oracle' attributed to Mary (9 November 1969) re-echoes the same theme. Thus the authorisation by Rome of what was an ancient practice in the Church was condemned and this dispute became one of the main arguments against San Damiano. There is no need to go into further details of this affair. Suffice it to say that Pope John Paul II is endeavouring to restore order and harmony by providing a proper pastoral service. This is the only substitute for sterile condemnation. I offer this case as an example of what happens when, because of rigid principles against apparitions, people are left to their own devices in a most delicate area that requires acceptance and guidance. In general people are only too willing to obey if they feel that an effort is being made to understand their views, their special grace and insight.

Freedom remains intact
The convergence of trends which tended to devalue apparitions

gave rise to the principles which are now current in this area. But we need to go beyond them. Take the following point of view, for example: as long as an apparition is not officially recognised by the Church we should not speak about it nor should we visit the place. We should wait. Otherwise one is acting imprudently, disrupting good order and disobeying the Church.

This is not the traditional position of the Church. At the time of the prophets and of Christ, indeed at any period in which apparitions and other charisms have arisen in the Church, the believing faithful have attended with open hearts and an open mind — though by no means uncritically. To the extent that the believing faithful recognised a divine action, they have been generous in the sense of obedience. This is what happened at Lourdes, Pontmain, Fatima, Beauraing, etc. All of this is perfectly normal.

If you hear that a dear friend is about to visit you from overseas you will meet that friend at the airport rather than saying: 'Perhaps it is a false rumour. Maybe the flight will be cancelled. I won't take the risk of making a mistake, of being disappointed.' For someone who really loves, this kind of attitude is out of the question. Love would prefer to be disappointed by the non-arrival of the expected loved one than to disappoint that loved one by being absent. This is the evidence of the heart. Arguments to the contrary have no place in a context of love. They simply promote indifference towards God, Christ and Our Lady.

To this we must add the urgency of certain messages proclaimed during these apparitions: the world is in great danger, be converted, etc. If an alarm bell rings within our hearing we do not say 'It is someone else's problem, leave it to the fire services'. In such cases we immediately contact the relevant authorities and render what assistance we can. It would be utter negligence to do otherwise.

Mgr Laurence, Bishop of Lourdes, and others have approved the promptness and generosity of the faithful in discerning the signs from heaven. The official recognition of the authenticity of the apparitions at Massabielle sees 'the throng of people' at the grotto as an argument in favour of the authenticity of the apparitions. Catherine Labouré and Don Bosco joyfully recognised these apparitions before Mgr Laurence did so. 'It is the same Virgin' said Catherine Labouré.

If, therefore, the people at the time had been guided by present-day strictures and ignored the apparitions, it would have been pointless for the Church to have investigated and approved them. The apparitions would have been still-born and the Church would have lost a great deal.

The discernment of the faithful and the judgment of the Church

Those who seek to prevent this normal exercise of the faith by ordinary people tend, on the other hand, to over-emphasise the judgement of authority as if it were infallible. Thus transfixed by infallibility, the faithful would have to withhold judgement before the decision, and later give consent, in both cases acting blindly. This is not the tradition of the Church. Apparitions and signs from heaven have always been issues of free choice. They are a call from God, always present, unlike the deaf and dumb idols ridiculed by the Psalmist (Ps 115:6; 135:17).

There is a very good reason for this apart altogether from the wisdom and circumspection of the Church. The magisterium speaks in the name of Christ and with his authority when it proclaims his revelation, the gospel. But when it comes to deciding on whether this or that cure is a miracle, the work of God, or whether it was indeed the Virgin who appeared to a visionary, then we are at a different level in the life of the Church. Expert commissions no doubt act with extreme care and caution in examining the context of each event. Nevertheless they cannot, as it were, touch the apparition itself. Their opinion remains conjectural. It is possible, but not infallible. For this reason, both before and after the Church's ruling, each Christian's freedom remains totally intact (though always within the bounds of good order, prudence and charity).

The Church is not made up of galley slaves. Its basic law is that of liberty in the Spirit. This liberty always triumphs when relations between pastors and faithful are enlivened by charity and obedience. The same Holy Spirit inspires humility and obedience equally.

Fr Estrate, who was spiritual director to the Carmelite convent in Bethlehem, was extremely worried about the extraordinary happenings that surrounded the life of Sister Mary of Jesus Crucified. One day he consulted with Alphonse Ratisbonne (the convert associated with the miraculous medal). Alphonse listened. He asked only one question:

'Is she obedient?'

'Oh', said Fr Estrate, 'As far as that is concerned, there is no problem, she is a model.'

'Then you may believe in her sanctity in spite of all the extraordinary happenings. I believe in it myself.' This little Sister is today beatified in spite of the extraordinary (divine and diabolical) events that continued to surround her life.

Genuine visionaries have an instinctive feeling for God's freedom and human liberty and an acute sense of obedience within which they grow and develop. Vicka, one of the visionaries of Medjugorje, was asked by pilgrims:

'How do you deal with those who do not believe in apparitions?' She replied (though she herself was totally convinced of the reality of Medjugorje):

'One is free to believe or not to believe in Medjugorje. The gospel does not say, ''You must believe'' … ''You must not believe''. We are all free' (Interview of 5 August 1987 in *Dernières Nouvelles,* no. 7, p. 78).

In another interview she was asked:

'How are sceptics to be convinced?'

'You will never convince them through words alone,' she replied. 'Don't even try. Your lifestyle, your love and your constant prayers for them will convince them of the reality which is central to your own life' (October 1987, in *Dernières Nouvelles,* no. 7, p. 76). The same serenity is evident in Mgr Franič's explanation of his disagreement with Mgr Žanič who had remained opposed to the apparitions (ibid).

Let us take the promptings of Vatican II seriously; let us try to go beyond a purely juridical mentality that would have believers reduced to robots in a permanent state of blind expectancy, practising blind obedience both before and after the Church's judgment: abstention before the judgment and submission after it. This passivity is diametrically opposed to the freedom of Christian life, because both the faithful and the authorities live by God's grace and the inspiration of the Spirit. These graces are shared through co-operation in the act of discernment. Problems are overcome by a little self-sacrifice on all sides, so that charity and obedience prevail in an atmosphere of openness and self-criticism.

The ambivalence of apparitions

We have seen that a paradoxical agreement of sorts has emerged between the left and certain members of the right in their opposition to apparitions. This in itself constitutes an invitation to find the middle ground in a Church in which there are too many tendencies to the right and the left.

The left is correct in living out the faith in the dark night of the soul, but sometimes it fails to attend to the stars which God places in this night: his signs and his power. There remains of course the temptation to overcompensate for the darkness and the void by over-commitment to practices which are at best described as 'activism', which lack the light and strength derived from contact with the living God. This was the experience of Alphonse Ratisbonne. Before his conversion through his vision of the miraculous medal, he was a pioneer in the society for the emancipation of Jews, which also included bishops, generals, ministers and industrialists. He found himself compensating for the radical secularisation of his Jewish faith, which had become almost extinct for him, by total commitment to social action on behalf of the poor of the Jewish community. He was afflicted with a confused sense of spiritual asphyxia, from which he was rescued by the apparition.

Members of a more right-wing tendency are correct in attending to signs from heaven, but they become centred on these exceptional tangible signs too readily. They overestimate the importance of these events and accept them with undue haste. Pilgrimages to places of apparitions abound, to the detriment of the more fundamental teachings of the Church and to the neglect of social and family obligations, of which the apparitions themselves are often a reminder. There is the danger of straying into a religion of apparitions. The tendency to the left frequently leads to asphyxia of the faith. The tendency to the right leads to superstition, illuminism and distortion of focus.

In order to avoid imbalance on either side we have to understand clearly not only the values of these extraordinary manifestations of the supernatural, but also their limitations. In many ways apparitions are an ambivalent phenomenon. Two important considerations have to be constantly borne in mind: apparitions are adapted to the visionaries and visionaries perceive them according to their own capacity.

On the one hand an apparition does not bestow the beatific vision on the visionaries. The visionaries are not taken up into heaven. Apparitions are a limited communication from heaven to earth. In that they are a prophetic call adapted to a given place in a given time they are authentic, but they do not purport to be an adequate expression of Christianity.

On the other hand, because this communication transcends the visionaries themselves, they have to receive it in a manner adapted to their abilities. Thus apparitions are marked by a double relativity.

1. Heavenly signs are adapted to humans. It is clear that the invisible God manifests himself in signs that are at once real and symbolic, such as the fire of the burning bush seen by Moses and in the sign seen by Pascal. Similarly, angels are not corporeal beings and therefore show themselves through signs. But we should not conclude from this that apparitions are purely subjective. All knowledge is communicated through signs which remain bound by relativity; human knowledge, after all, is never perfect or adequate. It is, of course, authentic when the sign is made known objectively and renders the communicator authentically present according to the means used, for example aurally by telephone or visually on a television screen.

The apparitions of Our Lady are marked by this same necessary adaptation of all knowledge. She speaks the language of the visionary: the local patois to Bernadette (which caused a certain amount of astonishment), Croatian in Medjugorje and Spanish in Latin America. In addition, Our Lady's clothing changes from one apparition to another. At Guadalupe her dress had a pattern of stylised flowers, a blue cloak covered with stars (in which astrologers discovered various constellations) and a sash of the type worn by pregnant women of the area. This was a sign of the incarnation given to Mexico. At rue du Bac she wore a snow white dress. A blue sash, caught at the front, is added at Lourdes. The clothing at la Salette (1846) is unusual. Here she wore the frilly bonnet and crimped dress of a peasant woman. At Medjugorje she wears a bright silver-grey, bluish dress which the visionaries are unable to describe accurately. A Belgian painter went to enormous trouble to reproduce a sample of what the garment might have looked like. The visionaries remained hesitant and embarrassed. 'No, you just cannot make it like it was', was Bernadette's comment.

What is the meaning of this variety in Our Lady's clothing? Is it a death blow to the reality of the apparitions? Must we inevitably conclude that the visionaries dress Our Lady in the clothes of the local peasant population or again in the manner of the statues they have seen in the church? But the clothes described in the apparitions bear only the remotest resemblance to what the locals wore at the time. The same is true of the statues which they would have seen. The variety is due in part to the details of the local communication. The clothing becomes a sign which elaborates and interprets the message. The white dress at Lourdes and rue du Bac signify Mary Immaculate, the stars on the blue background at Guadalupe and Pontmain speak of heaven. More particularly, the crown of stars at Guadalupe, rue du Bac and Medjugorje indicate the woman of the Apocalypse, clothed in the sun and crowned with a crown of twelve stars, who comes down from heaven to attend the painful birth of a new world.

There is a further disturbing aspect: the Virgin Mary is not always the same age. To Teresa of Avila she appeared as a young girl and, in varying degrees, as a young girl to Bernadette and (once) to Bernardo, the visionary of Cuapa. This was meant to underline the Immaculate Conception as expressed by Bernanos: 'A little girl, queen of the angels, younger than sin and younger than the world which begot her'. In other instances the visionaries, with some hesitation, compare her to a woman between sixteen and eighteen years old, even to a thirty-year-old woman — never, to my knowledge, older than this. Mary always appears to be young, because eternity is youth.

Does this go against all objectivity? Indeed not, as this may well be the property of glorified bodies. Will the person who died at the age of 100 always appear old and doddering or will that person revert to his or her prime? The mystery of life in God transcends the possibilities of our earth-bound imagination; It destroys the bonds of servitude that tie us to flesh and escapes the limits imposed by time; eternity liberates us from these dimensions. Eternal life marks a transition to an existence that freezes all things in their prime; it perpetuates youth. Thus Our Lady can be contemporary to any period and can appear at any age she chooses.

A scientist who was working with me at Medjugorje suggested that we might verify the authenticity of the apparitions there by comparing the description given by the visionaries with the imprint of the face left by Our Lady on the cloak of the visionary at Guadalupe. I responded that such a procedure would get us nowhere.

We do not know the extent to which a sign can be adapted. Many surmised that Our Lady would be seen as an African if she were to appear in Africa. But the visionaries of Kibeho, at least at first sight, did not confirm this. The vision which they saw transcended all racial characteristics. Apparitions continue to confound our ideological scheme of things. While there is enormous diversity in the various descriptions, some features do remain constant in all apparitions, from Lourdes to Medjugorje: Our Lady's youth, her smile, her sadness when speaking about sin, her motherly tenderness and her blue eyes.

2. The relativity and diversity of the apparitions also depends on the visionary, the subject who receives them — 'All things are received according to the possibilities of the recipient' *(quidquid recipitur ad modum recipientis recipitur),* according to the dictum of Thomas Aquinas. In very ordinary terms, we are incapable of tuning into the same sound waves as birds that hunt in the night. The means of sensory knowledge are varied and each one is limited to some extent. If someone from the other world decides to communicate with us, the person who receives this communication does so with the means at his or her disposal. When speaking about this communication the visionary is bound by the limitations of language and is aware of its inadequacy.

The function of apparitions is not to deliver an absolute communication, but a limited one. In this regard the word of the visionary does not enjoy the same status as the words of scripture, the Word of God expressed in human terms by a human author. A visionary gives a limited, filtered, conditioned account of a divine communication, which is not guaranteed in the same way as the inspired authors of the Bible.

More needs to be said on this point. In this world an act of knowing can never be reduced to pure intuition. It is the act of a subject who normally leaves his own imprint on this act without jeopardising the objectivity of his knowledge. We must be wary of falling into the trap of idealism: God, Christ and the Virgin really exist. We can meet them, they can communicate with us in the real sense of the word. All communication has a subjective dimension in so far as it is the act of a subject, but it is also objective, to the degree to which it puts us in touch with the object. God, Christ and the Virgin have given us various means of reaching them objectively, such as pure faith and, exceptionally, apparitions, a 'viaticum' on the road back to God. They get in touch with us in the circumstances in which we find ourselves on this earth. Obviously, none of this knowledge is adequate (i.e. capable of adequately encompassing the object). While we must recognise the relativity of apparitions, we should not exaggerate it. We should not over-emphasise one aspect to the detriment of another.

For genuine visionaries an apparition is a personal encounter and of itself provides evidence more convincing than any other. 'I see and I cannot say the opposite', was Bernadette's constant refrain, in spite of threats from the authorities.

When the apparitions are over the visionaries return to the ordinary world. This is not like waking after a dream, when reality blots out the vagueness of the dream. The visionaries return to the vagueness and vicissitudes of an uncertain world.

Recognition of the ambivalence of apparitions is not a reason for rejecting them. All that we know and experience in this world is ambivalent, subject to the law of change. From birth to death we cope with ambiguity, negotiating the hazards of school, work, marriage, children — each of them bringing us face to face with problems which have to be solved for better or for worse. We have no choice. We are not in a position to say: 'I refuse to be born and to die. I do not accept school, work, marriage, children or celibacy for the sake of the kingdom.'

We are tossed on the waves of these ambiguities. We are forced into making choices that tear us apart. Moral theologians tell us that whereas truth is unequivocal, human behaviour (morality) offers the choice of several equal solutions.

Growth and evolution, the ingredients of life and history, are ambivalent, but this very ambivalence leads to its own solutions. The ambivalence of apparitions rests on the fact that they are signs given in the obscurity of faith. They are a tangible light, signs of a fleeting encounter with the Lord or his holy mother, who make themselves visibly present. They are a limited manifestation of heaven to those who are on earth, making their way towards heaven.

A further ambivalence emerges from the status afforded them by the Church. Their certainty is not guaranteed as is, for example, the certainty of the Credo. The reason for this is that we are not dealing with part of the essential message God confided to the Church, but with a single event in the history of the Church. This single event does not have the same importance in the life of the Church. So it is that the Church has not been given the charism to recognise it infallibly. The Church is aware (and the Councils since Lateran V bear witness to this) that its judgment in these matters is always the result of painful discernment, aided by panels of experts, who carefully examine all the scientific and spiritual parameters of each phenomenon before deciding on its authenticity.

For this reason the Church's judgment on these events does not engage her infallibility. When the Church recognises the authenticity of an apparition she does not say: 'The Virgin has appeared here and you are obliged to believe it!' Rather, the recognition means: 'There are good reasons for you to believe. It would be beneficial and fruitful and we invite you to believe— but without an obligation to faith!'

It is for this very reason that the popes have not become arbiters of authenticity. The matter is left to the local prelate, even when the events have a universal dimension. Popes may well confirm and have confirmed the judgment of the local bishop. Indeed in the case of Paul VI and John Paul II, as well as encouraging the faithful to visit Fatima, they went there themselves. Pius XII had wished to visit Lourdes on 15 August (1958)—as his successor John Paul II later did without formally involving the authority of the Church.

Apparitions do not, therefore, enjoy that degree of certainty which is proper to dogmas of faith. As a result of scrutiny and discernment they are recognised with a more or less high degree of probability. This is not equivalent to saying that they are doubtful. History and science abound in truths which do not enjoy absolute certitude, but which are sufficiently grounded to allow us to act on them in spite of the possibility of human error (*errare humanum est* — to err is human).

Dogmas and apparitions exist at different levels in our life of faith. They do not have the same vital importance. Total adherence to the Word of God is necessary for salvation. Adherence to this or that apparition is not necessary.

Can we be certain?
It does not follow that in the case of apparitions we can never be certain.

— The visionaries themselves may well be granted the grace of absolute certainty regarding the apparitions they have received. It was so with Bernadette in the period during which she was called on to witness to the apparitions. Paradoxically, God withdrew this certainty from her during the long night of temptation that was to mark the final painful period of her existence.

— Those who have close contact with the visionaries, particularly priests who daily witness the action of grace in the sacrament of penance, may also be given the grace of personal certainty.

— Certainty may be the result of expert investigations through which other possible hypotheses have been eliminated, but beware; these experts remain private individuals and have no official authority. They would in fact be going beyond this brief if they were to assume any of the functions of the magisterium. Their personal convictions do not allow them to judge or to impose their views.

This is a delicate situation in which I, as an expert, find myself. I have reached firm conclusions (concerning Medjugorje) which I constantly review. My conviction is as valuable as the reasons I give to support it. But, curiously enough, when a bishop officially recognises an apparition he bases his judgment on reasons for believing that emerge after careful examination. He too shares these with the faithful. But he does this with the official authority of the Church, assisted in his episcopal function by the help of the Holy Spirit. This is a major difference. His views require obedience in principle.

When the Bishop of Mostar announced (in *Positio* and in various interviews) that he would shortly be giving a negative judgment on Medjugorje, I had already clearly foreseen this eventuality (*Dernières Nouvelles* 3, pp. 22-23 and pp. 56-62). Given the bishop's case, if he does go ahead and give a negative judgment, I will adopt an attitude of discretion and obedience to whatever falls under his edicts. But, at the same time, I will feel obliged, as did those who knew Joan of Arc (condemned as a relapsed heretic by a tribunal of the Church), to prepare a revision of the errors. But it has not come to this. The case was taken out of Mgr Žanič hands and passed to higher authority.[4]

Notes

1. While the Bible denounces false prophets it also denounces the systematic suppression of prophetism (Am 2:11-12; Is 30:10; cf. Jr 11:21; Zc 1:5; Ne 9:30) which, to the detriment of the people of God, has the effect of extinguishing the prophetic vision and function (Lm 2:9-10; cf. Ezk 3:26; Ps 74:9; cf. 77:9; Dn 3:38). It would appear that in the Bible and in the Church suppression of prophets and visionaries persisted until it succeeded and then the tone changed to a lament that visions and prophecy no longer occurred (1 S 3:1; 1 M 9:27). The reappearance of the gift of prophecy is among the promises made in respect of the restoration of Israel (Is 59:21: Ho 12:10-11; Jl 2:28-32); this situation continues in the New Testament (Mt 23:37; Ac 2:16-18). See W. Vogels, 'Il n'y aura plus de prophètes!' *Nouvelle Revue Théologique,* 1979, pp. 844-859).

2. René Laurentin, *Un amour extraordinaire: Yvonne-Aimée de Malestroit,* Œil, 1985, followed by: *Écrits et prédictions de Soeur Yvonne-Aimée,* ibid, 1986.

3. These trends, which were not without coherence and insight, represented for many the downfall of religious, moral and spiritual values and laid the foundations for modern atheism. One of the significant cultural turning points in this evolution was the reappearance of idealism (Hegel) in the guise of materialism (Feuerbach and Marx). Idealism reduces matter to spirit. Materialism does quite the opposite; it reduces spirit to matter. Marx and Lenin gave the system a coherence and a logic. But materialism and idealism are the result of undue simplification. They are like the obverse sides of a coin. Their common denominator is the fact that they both neglect the dynamic tension between matter and spirit, between knowledge and subject. This tension is the cornerstone of realism, the only philosophical system that is in harmony with Christianity, with the Incarnation.

Idealism was at the root of many of the doubts (not only about apparitions) among certain theologians who were frequently unaware of their philosophical presuppositions and of the influence of these presuppositions on their understanding of the faith. While idealism continues to have a strong influence in universities, even in Catholic universities, the influence of Marxist materialism is more limited. An example of the latter might be the various 'liberation theologies' and the small circle of materialistic exegesis. F. Belo's interpretation of Mark's Gospel according to the principles of Marx made headlines.

4. Briefly, where apparitions are concerned, personal certainty may co-exist with an absence of official certainty even when there is official recognition. Some theologians were of the view that Lourdes was infallibly recognised, not as dogma but as a dogmatic fact. But the very idea of 'dogmatic fact' is itself ambivalent and widely discussed. The view proposed at the International Mariological Congress in Lourdes in 1958 has not gained ground (René Laurentin in *Revue des sciences philosophiques et théologiques,* 48, 1964, pp. 115-120 and *Sur les routes de Dieu,* Œil, 1984, pp. 125-127).

3

HOW CAN THE AUTHENTICITY OF APPARITIONS BE ASSESSED?

Is it possible to answer the question raised by Cardinal Sin and by many other Christians: What does Our Lady want to tell the world? This question is concerned only with those apparitions that are most in evidence nowadays. It is also worth noting that these apparitions of the Virgin also refer to and are frequently accompanied by apparitions of Christ. We will see this particularly at Damascus, Medjugorje, Kibeho and San Nicolas.

The question presupposes a double line of enquiry:

1. Where are the authentic apparitions of the Virgin taking place? It is only in the light of this first question that we can approach the second:
2. What is she saying to us?

Where is the Virgin appearing?
In answering the first question we are guided by criteria that have been developed by the Church over the years and updated by a confidential document from the Congregation of the Faith (25 February 1978):

1. *Sufficiency of information:* This is still not available for Grouchevo in the USSR (Ukraine[1]) and for many others, particularly in Italy[2] and in Nigeria.[3]

2. *Orthodoxy:* Do the apparitions conform with faith and morals? A serious error in this respect would jeopardise their authenticity: 'Every kingdom divided against itself is laid waste' (Mt 12:25; Mk 3:24).

3. *Transparency:* Do the apparitions and visionaries lead us to God, to Christ, to the gospel, to the service of God and humanity and to the promotion of faith, good order and peace? Or are they self-promoting, emphasising the peculiarities of their choices and their vision, the tumult of their inspirations and the esoteric nature of their rites, etc?

4. *Signs:* Are there serious reasons for believing in the presence of the hand of God, as Mgr Laurence put it, in cures, conversions and other miracles, such as the dance of the sun at Fatima and other signs from heaven?

5. *Expert opinion:* Do experts of various disciplines (especially doctors and psychiatrists) believe that the visionaries, particularly during ecstasy, are healthy or pathological?

I am aware that this final criterion is still under discussion. The first scientific studies of the mentally ill were carried out by Charcot and Janet, both rationalists. In the case of hysterics, they inferred a state of disconnectedness. Some theologians, perhaps influenced by rationalism and out of respect for science, have swallowed this line. They believed ecstasy to be a pathological state and concluded that God, all powerful, may have used this pathological state to make himself manifest. We cannot exclude the possibility that God would manifest himself to sick people, even mentally ill people, in a personal way. God despises no one and his mercy extends to all.

But these graces, given essentially for the consolation of the ill, are not exemplary. Some theologians who discover abnormal cases which are significant or instructive, are only too inclined to raise them to the status of examples. Thus, classical theology used the case of baptism, received in a state of mortal sin, simply to emphasise its infallible efficacy *ex opere operato*. But this is not the normal case. It is marginal and regrettable. In the same way, if God wishes to manifest himself to a mentally ill person, his grace will not necessarily confirm that person in his or her pathological state. It will improve that person's situation, bring about a partial cure as divine providence sees fit. Judgment in these matters is often faulty. When Charcot diagnosed ecstasy (i.e. lack of contact with the outside world), he exploited and aggravated the hysteria, but not for the good of the hysteric.

6. *Do these apparitions bear good fruit?* The sixth criterion is the principal and decisive one since it is Christ himself who laid it down: Do these apparitions bear good fruit, or not? Again theological fascination with extreme cases has led to the following principle: visions are granted to visionaries not for their own benefit but for others. It matters little, then, if the visionary is

a sinner; his function is to transmit signs and messages to others. This is a classical thesis. But the constant experience of the Church makes it clear that we are dealing, not with a normal case, but rather with an extreme (and regrettable) one. St Paul emphasises that 'He who speaks in tongues edifies himself' *(1 Co 14:4)*. If the visionary proves to be unbalanced or a sinner, the mission which has been confided to him by God will undoubtedly suffer and this ought to be seen as a negative indication. If on the other hand, as in the cases of Bernadette and Catherine Labouré, the visionary is sanctified by these apparitions, there is a strong positive argument. The fruits of an apparition must therefore be judged on a number of levels: the visionaries themselves; the evidence of their lives which, when it reflects the message, is frequently eloquent, Bernadette being a case in point; the surroundings, the pilgrims and all those who believe in the apparitions and visit the visionaries.

7. *Is the Church authority favourable or unfavourable?* Although, as we pointed out, the Church does not take advantage of its infallibility in these matters, its qualified judgment does take on particular importance. It is normally decisive in respect of the first criterion: the strict authority of the Church can exclude an apparition on grounds of non-conformity with faith and morals. This judgment always requires respect and obedience.

Even with the help of these valuable criteria I still feel immensely presumptuous in attempting an interpretation of current apparitions, which are, in fact, difficult to judge. Who is in a position to judge apparitions world-wide, when each local bishop is, in fact, standing back from the situation, careful not to compromise his authority; when the Congregation of the Faith, faced with a plethora of apparitions, maintains that wise discretion which its official position requires; when the popes themselves have always been careful not to act in an official capacity, in order to avoid confusion between infallibility and the conjectural nature of judgments on apparitions? For this reason John Paul II is content to exchange discreet directives with the Congregation of the Faith and with various experts, never actually taking a position, but constantly praying that discernment will prevail.

While the authorities have to exercise caution in these matters an expert can take some risks. All that is at stake is his reputation and the reasons he presents for and against the case. Both sides of the story have to be presented fairly.

In many cases the balance will come down on the negative side, without however attaching any blame to those who in good faith may have been misled. (see Appendix 4, Apparitions without credibility, pp. 139).

An examination of even one apparition requires an immense amount of work. I spent more than twenty years working on Lourdes; five on Pontmain; nine years on the Miraculous Medal—and in all of these I had the help of a team of collaborators. I came to understand that in each of these apparitions vast areas of scepticism remained, even within the institutions which benefited, even though these discreet doubts were not considered sinful by the Church. Indeed, even when apparitions were recognised by the Church, there remained on the the margins areas of discernment between the essential authenticity of the events and human frailty—even sinfulness—from which the visionaries are not preserved. Medjugorje involved me in eighteen different trips and thousands of hours of work. In the case of the other apparitions, on which I did not have as much time to spend, I am naturally aware of the limitations and indeed the relativity of my overall judgment. The request from Cardinal Sin is not my only reason for persevering with this work. The Congregation of the Faith welcomes and encourages preparatory work by experts. *The Congregation's Norms in the matter of procedures and of judging presumed apparitions and private revelations* (25 February 1978) formally set out the conditions in which the Pope may intervene. This may happen when the local judgment is in error or in other ways incomplete. Furthermore, the Pope may intervene at the request of a group of qualified faithful *(coetus qualificatus fidelium)*.

In this the Congregation is ratifying its own experience. It has discovered that expert groups of genuinely competent theologians and scientists have allowed it to reappraise shortcomings in local judgment. It was precisely because of the evidence of such experts that final judgment was taken out of the hands of the Bishop of Mostar on the occasion of his visit to Rome to convey his negative view of Medjugorje. The Congregation has been furnished with certain documents by French and Italian doctors and theologians proving the seriousness of Medjugorje and the importance of not extinguishing the Spirit (1 Th 5:19).

Judgment and pastoral care

The document which emanated from the Congregation of the Faith has contributed enormously to greater clarity in the tangled question of apparitions. This has not been without its consequences.

Given the recent burgeoning of apparitions one might wonder why the Congregation did not pursue the same policy as Cardinal Ottaviani when he dealt with a similar situation during the Second World War: apparitions, predictions, opinions were all tactfully suppressed. Perhaps there is not the same degree of illuminism now as there was during that period. Hence, while being careful to be well-informed, Rome no longer rushes in to dissuade and suppress. Moreover, the document prepared under the direction of Cardinal Seper draws a very important distinction between judgment and pastoral care in the matter of apparitions.

All possible scientific means must be used in arriving at a judgment. The document encourages this. But one can never forget that apparitions represent a phenomenon of faith in the midst of the people of God and that the visionaries involved in these phenomena ought to benefit from pastoral care for better and not for worse. This was Cardinal Ratzinger's reply to Vittorio Messon's questions about the impressive proliferation of assumed apparitions. He proposes the following distinction:

> One of our decisive criteria is not to confuse a judgment on the supernatural truth of the events with a judgment on their *spiritual fruits.* It is only recently that we have begun to use scientific categories in our attempts to reach a judgment on these manifestations. One could not establish *scientifically* the historic truth of certain traditions on the basis of which the Middle Ages built some of its more venerable sanctuaries. This has not prevented pilgrimages to such places from being fruitful, beneficial and important in the Christian life. The real problem is not, therefore, modern hypercriticism (which in its own way gives rise to a new type of credulity) but, rather, the evaluation of the vitality and the orthodoxy of the religious life which develops in these places.

Father Gianni Sgreva wished to establish a community which would live out the message of Medjugorje, but wondered if it was not premature given that the Church had not officially recognised the apparitions. Cardinal Ratzinger's reply was: Do not worry about the *facts,* we will worry about them. Look after the results, the *fruits.*

This important distinction between judgment on the facts (the authenticity of the apparition) and judgment on the fruits had the further effect of a distinction in Cardinal Seper's document between two stages or even two functions in the episcopal judgment: pastoral recognition of the fruits and authentication of the facts.

After the first global examination of the facts (which might require urgency rather than caution), if nothing is found contrary to faith and morals, if the apparitions are seen to produce good fruit, the bishops may officially authorise the cult without pronouncing on the authenticity of the apparition. Things may well remain there. Such is the case at Pellevoisin or at rue du Bac. These apparitions have never been the subject of an official judgment.

This is the solution recently adopted in the Pope's own diocese at Tre Fontane, where a place of pilgrimage had existed since 1949. Beginning on 12 April 1947 Bruno Cornacchiolo (a fanatic Adventist) had been the beneficiary of several apparitions of the Blessed Virgin. She dissuaded Bruno from murdering the Pope, Pius XII, at whose feet a repentant Bruno laid down his arms on 8 December 1949. Rome had wisely channelled the pilgrims to a sanctuary in the care of enlightened religious. In the spring of 1987 the Cardinal Vicar of Rome (the Pope's official episcopal representative for the diocese) celebrated mass at Tre Fontane and did not even once mention the apparition, which had never been officially recognised. The cult, not the supernatural character of the apparition, is officially recognised. We ought to be mindful of these distinctions in our enjoyment of the generous freedom accorded us by the Church in respect of apparitions. This freedom must be governed by prudence and must be attentive to the good order of the Church.

I am therefore aware of the difficulties of arriving at a proper discernment of these events, a discernment which is vital if one is to overcome the radical opposition which divides the Church in these matters: credulity on the one hand and suppression on the other and the reciprocal animosity between both camps. The third way, that of discernment, is despised and misunderstood.

It is caught up in the crossfire between the left and the right. No doubt I will get caught in the same crossfire. If in one or other of the apparitions I discover light and good pastoral results, critics of the ideologies will say: 'He has stepped into credulity. He is no longer acting as a theologian.' Then, if in the other apparitions I bring to the fore a degree of uncertainty, ambiguity or even deviation, no doubt I will be censured by the credulous.

For example, 'Little Pebble' (an adult Australian atheist convert, inspired by pious messages for this sinful world) allowed himself to be swayed from grace into the realms of subjectivity and published the following message which he attributed to Our Lord (No. 150, dated 19 June 1987):

> Rest assured....you will be the real and only successor to John Paul II and you will be called Peter the Roman, Peter II. You will not be elected as the other Popes have been, but according to divine plans for the last Pope... you will reign until the end of time... An anti-Pope will seal himself on the throne of Peter after the death of Pope John Paul II, and his name is Casaroli, a demon worshipper. I make this known to you directly, my son, so that the entire Church may know it.... (*Recueil des messages,* p. 376).

When I wrote to the person who had kindly sent me these messages to be careful, as it was deviation, the only answer I received was: 'You do not want to believe, so I will no longer send you any messages. Your disbelief makes you unworthy.'

I would not say that Little Pebble is a diabolical personage. Without knowing him sufficiently I might have been disposed to believe in the authenticity of his conversion and perhaps of his early dialogues with heaven. What had led him astray? I did not have time to investigate. But it is clear that we are dealing with deviation.

It is curious to note that, without knowing it, he shared the same illusions (perhaps due to some experience with the established authorities of the Church?) as the deviations expressed by the so-called visionary of Bayside, New York, where the lady in question spread the following message: 'The man who presents himself as Paul VI is not the real Pope. The Pope has been imprisoned by his two principal collaborators, Cardinal Villot and Mgr Benelli, and they have substituted a double — the result of plastic surgery.

The man we are seeing is not the Pope.' This so-called 'revelation' was illustrated by two photographs: one a picture of an older Paul VI, taken in a moment of anxiety, and the other a younger, touched-up picture, that had virtually eliminated all wrinkles. It was obviously a fake.

I do not want to cast the first stone. But what a pity that Little Pebble and the visionary of Bayside did not have the benefit of the advice of a good spiritual director who would have enabled them to unravel the genuine motions of the Spirit from their own flights of fancy. It would have been of benefit to all concerned.

Both Cardinal Ratzinger and the Congregation of the Faith are absolutely right in emphasising the importance of pastoral care and spiritual direction in dealing with these unusual phenomena of apparitions, extraordinary charisms and prophetic missions. Merely looking at them from the outside without the benefit of pastoral care could lead to deviations and abuses. The Church's mission is to make grace more widespread, enlighten the uncertain, strengthen the weak and heal the sinner. It is as well to set out this basic truth from the outset and it will also be our principal conclusion.

What is Our Lady saying?

There remains the second question: What is Our Lady saying to us? To what degree can we trust the message that is transmitted in the case of the few chosen events whose credibility seems more apparent? (This does not mean that we exclude cases about which we have less data.) The same Thomistic principle applies here also: 'Whatever is received is received according to the measure of the recipient', including the recipient's participation and involvement and sometimes their own failures, interpretations and exaggerations.

The interpretation of apparitions is more complex than the interpretation of inspired Scripture which is the Word of God. Visionaries represent a more or less transparent, fragile medium. Their messages, unlike the Scriptures, are not the Word of God and the difference is paramount. Nor are they infallible, as are the teachings of the Pope when he speaks *ex cathedra*. There are no short cuts in this delicate matter of arriving at a decision. Even the Pope himself, with the special graces attached to his office and the availability to him of numerous experts, still experiences problems.

One single example illustrates these problems. The apparitions at Fatima are foremost among those which enjoy official recognition, rivalled only by Lourdes. Two Popes went as pilgrims to Fatima. However, dialogue between the visionary Lucia and the last six Popes has been difficult. Ever since the 1930s she has requested them to consecrate Russia to the Immaculate Heart of Mary. Pius XI and John XXIII did not accede to this request. Pius XII, Paul VI and John Paul II have renewed the act of consecration on eight different occasions, each time adding further precisions at the request of Lucia. But Russia remains unconverted and Lucia feels that the often repeated act of consecration has not been done 'as the Virgin wished it'. No doubt, we are only at the beginning of the discussions of these matters.

A certain amount of tension remains between Lucia (the details of whose requests have varied from time to time) and the Pope, who is not infallible in this matter. Outspoken commentators haven't helped the situation. It might well be asked if the year consecrated to Mary, marking the millennium of Christianity in Russia, was not motivated by a desire to satisfy a request of Our Lady of Fatima.

The difficulty in the relationship between Lucia and the Pope can be interpreted in three ways:

1. According to some devotees of Fatima, the popes who did not obey Lucia are responsible for the persecutions and deaths which continue in the USSR. These individuals then go on either to accuse or excuse the Pope.

2. The consecration has been carried out. The conversion of Russia has begun. Conversions among the younger generation, who have been educated according to atheistic principles, are growing evidence of this. They point to people like Tatiana Goritcheva and her associates, who founded a new feminist movement in Russia in 1980.

3. Finally, those theologians who are more critical of apparitions are of the view that these endless renewals of acts of consecration are positive proof that the popes were wrong in involving their

high office at the behest of individual apparitions. In listening to a visionary they degraded their magisterium, neither converting Russia nor satisfying the visionary.

Thus if the popes' involvement, even after reflection on the results of wide-ranging investigations, coupled with the exceptional sense of discernment of the head of the Church, has given rise to such discussions that the faithful are allowed to believe or not in these matters, then we can see how difficult it is to discern the meaning and import of a given message.

Successive popes have hesitated over Lucia's request. Though the apparitions enjoyed ample official approval, Lucia herself remained hesitant as to the modality of many of the messages she received. Visionaries may well experience difficulty in distinguishing what they received from God from what they themselves contribute to the experience — their normal active effort to take cognisance of the message and formulate it. The visionaries' contribution may be greater or smaller depending on whether they receive intelligible messages or expressions in clear words. The ordinary human frailty of the visionaries may also have an influence. Bernadette was so traumatised by her first visit to Peyramale that she was never able to recall the exact words of the message relating to the procession.

In the wide area of the ambiguity of apparitions the prophetic element is particularly ambiguous and subject to the limitations of an individual's current standpoint. The proximity of the kingdom of God, towards which we are all tending, may appear very close to the person who ardently desires its coming. The summit of a mountain sometimes appears so close that it could be touched even from the foothills and yet during a long and painful climb this same summit will often disappear from view. The end to which God calls us is perpetually imminent. In the earliest of the Epistles, Paul believed he would see Christ's second coming before his own death (1 Th 4:17).

It should not therefore surprise us that visionaries sometimes have this same standpoint. While this view may well heighten fervour and vigilance, we should not see this revelation of imminence as meaning proximity in time. While visionaries may see angels this does not entitle us to conclude that angels are visible corporal beings. They may well see the elect in heaven or even the damned in hell, they may even describe the colour of their garments, yet we should not conclude (following the dubious thesis of certain theologians) that the resurrection of the body has already taken place. All these matters serve as an indicator of the relativity of apparitions. Our study points to differences between apparitions of Christ or the Virgin, who can appear in their glorious bodies. But when they do, we must examine the mysteriously specific nature of this communication. We should not use the image of some ship from outer space, because Christ and Mary do not belong to our dimensions of space or time, but to the eternity of God. Glorious bodies do not have to overcome the barrier of distance in space but, rather, the chasm that divides eternity from time. For this reason, even when an apparition of the Virgin shows strong signs of objectivity (rue du Bac, Lourdes, Medjugorje), the act of perceiving shows characteristics that differ from those of ordinary perception. The others who are present at the apparition do not, in fact, see it. An apparition is not perceived through the ordinary material channels of communication. At Medjugorje both the eyes and the ears of the visionaries continue to receive stimuli from the outside world. These stimuli reach the cortex. And yet this contact with the outside world is somehow interrupted and they are only aware of the apparition. Perhaps they are dreaming? No, the electroencephalogram proves that they were neither asleep nor dreaming. The end of the apparition is not for them an awakening, a return to reality, but a return to the less real. These brief indications would suggest that what is at stake is a more direct, more immediate communication: a person-to-person existential communication which is totally possible for God, Christ and Our Lady.

Evidence and the twilight zone
We have underlined the limitations of apparitions and the consequent prudence with which we must approach them. It is the only way to reconcile enthusiasts with those who systematically oppose apparitions.

Though his or her communications with Christ or Our Lady are clear and evident, the visionary is often overwhelmed by this mystery. He or she is not adequately equipped to formulate the message nor is the visionary an ideal interpreter of the message. Divine manifestations, apparitions and miracles remain mysterious even for the visionary, who is incapable of giving an adequate account of them. Outside witnesses find themselves in an even more embarrassing position. Believers, commissioned experts and bishops have not had first-hand experience; they study the matter hesitatingly and from the outside, from the other side of a barrier. God shows himself here below in a twilight zone, not in the clear light of day. These tangible manifestations, though often striking, never provide mathematical certainty. They remain open to objections. There are no absolute proofs. Our freedom is not interfered with. Even in the most striking cases, such as Paul on the road to Damascus, our freedom is not removed. Apparitions are signs of love and in the context of love, they may well be gratifyingly evident. Happy are those who, within the Church, in obedience and humility, have had this experience of the presence and the power of God, of the closeness of Christ and his mother, our mother, who are so near to our minds and bodies.

The above observations ought to make it clear that our judgement in these matters will rise above the realms of the simplistic and naive. Thus we will approach the heart of the matter critically, while also being open to God's familiarity with us. I will present an overview of present-day apparitions and then, more precisely, examine those which, after preliminary investigations, meet the criteria laid down by the Church, while at the same time awaiting further data and remaining respectful of the judgment of the Church.

Notes

1. See Appendix 1, pp. 133-138.
2. Roccia del Paso and elsewhere.
3. The Bishop of Enegu has a negative attitude towards the visions of Servus Mariae.

PART II

Overview of present-day apparitions

1

AROUND THE WORLD

Cua, Betania (Venezuela) 1976-84

On a farm in Betania (in the village of Cua in the state of Miranda, Venezuela), two hours from Caracas, beside a grotto set on a hillside, the Virgin appeared to Maria Esperanza Medrano de Bianchini, the owner of the farm, born on 22 November 1928.

Maria was a pious woman of a mystical disposition. At the age of twelve she contracted bronchial pneumonia. Contrary to the doctors' pessimistic diagnosis, she made a mysterious recovery. She then became preoccupied with the religious life and entered the Franciscan order at Merida. But in 1954 she had an unexpected apparition of St Thérèse of the Child Jesus, who told her:

> This is not your vocation; you ought not become a nun, but work out your salvation as a wife and mother; this is your way to sanctification and bearing witness in the world.

On 1 November she met her future husband in Rome, in circumstances which had been indicated in the apparition. The marriage took place on 8 December 1956 in the chapel of the Immaculate Conception in St Peter's Basilica, with Mgr Giulio Rossi, parish priest of the Basilica, presiding. She had seven children — six girls and one boy—all of whom are married.

Maria was a devoted wife and mother. She continued to enjoy special charismatic graces which the bishop examined: clairvoyance, foretelling the future, levitations, transfiguration, stigmata, the gift of healing, the mysterious reception of communion and the mysterious emission of sweet-smelling odours of perfume and flowers. The Virgin appeared to Maria for the first time on 25 March 1976 beside a spring above the grotto:

> My daughter, I have given you my heart. I give it to you and will always give it to you.

She was given a mission of kindness and fidelity, service and sacrifice with the following assurance:

I will be your refuge.

The Virgin was bathed in light and said to Maria Esperanza:

I am the reconciler of all people.

There were further apparitions on 25 March 1977 and 25 March 1978. Still more were announced during which Mary would allow herself to be seen by others.[1]

This happened occasionally during the sporadic apparitions which took place subsequently and especially on the feast of the Annunciation, 25 March 1984. After Mass that day the crowds were beginning to relax when suddenly the Virgin appeared to them above the waterfall. The apparition was brief, but it was repeated seven times in the course of the afternoon. Each time it lasted from five to ten minutes: the final apparition lasted half an hour. Very many different types of people witnessed renewed apparitions; young and old, priests and laity. Most of them were poor and young (there was a large number of students from Caracas). But the bishop also discovered among them policemen and soldiers, doctors, psychologists, psychiatrists, engineers and lawyers. People who went on outings or picnics to Finca Betania also saw the Blessed Virgin: 'At least 500 to 1,000 people, but, in my opinion more than 1,000', according to the bishop (p. 4 of his *Presentation*). They see the apparition without experiencing trance or ecstasy and they don't lose contact with the outside world.

The Virgin does not appear in a stereotypical fashion. According to various witnesses she resembles Our Lady of Lourdes with her blue sash, but she also resembles the image on the Miraculous Medal; others describe her as Our Lady of Mount Carmel or Our Lady of Sorrows. The visionaries wonder about this diversity. Some believe that Our Lady is teaching us how to invoke her and understand her role in relation to the human race.

She is bathed in light, appears suddenly and is accompanied by the sweet perfume of roses and other phenomena. From March 1984 the crowds grew larger and the apparitions became more numerous, particularly on Saturdays, Sundays and feast days. In his letter of 7 April 1988 the bishop of the diocese (Los Teques) wrote to me: 'At the time of writing the most recent apparition took place one month ago on 7 March.'

This bishop, Mgr Pio Ricardo, undertook the investigation himself. As a Jesuit he had a good theological background, and had qualified in the ecclesiastical faculty of Oña (Burgos, Spain). He had written a doctoral thesis on psychology and taught this subject in the Central University of Caracas. He had an interest in mystical phenomena. His inquiry was methodical. He himself met the witnesses in their own surroundings. He questioned 490 people (some of them in groups) and put together a file of 381 written statements. The witnesses, from very different walks of life, appeared to him to be serious, sincere and basically in agreement with each other. The crowds, the intensity of the prayer and the remarkable fruits of conversion, prayer and cures are all present at Finca Betania:

> Those who come to the apparitions are greatly strengthened in their faith and spirituality. Their Christian lives improve. People who had never prayed now regularly recite the rosary. Those who never went to church now come regularly and avail of the sacraments of Penance and the Eucharist. There were remarkable conversions. Those who heard confessions at this place (myself included) will bear witness to this. All admit that they have experienced an interior change.... The apparitions have brought them close to God and renewed their Christian life.... Either through prayer, or the water from the waterfall there have been not only spiritual graces but extraordinary physical cures. Among these latter were the disappearance of advanced cancer of the kidneys and the sudden cure of two duodenal ulcers; the disappearance of an ovarian fibroma without recourse to the operation which had been judged indispensable and the unexpected cure of a vaginal mycosis which had resisted all treatment. I have obtained certification, diagnoses, analyses and proofs of a medical nature in three of the above-mentioned cases.

The apparitions have engendered a search for God and for the interior life, openness and obedience to the Church, solidarity and fraternal sharing. As a consequence, Mgr Ricardo has welcomed Our Lady's request to build a church to Our Lady the Reconciler of Peoples. A site was donated for the building. Having informed Rome, on 21 November 1987 he declared officially:

Having studied the apparitions of the Virgin Mary at Finca Betania and having prayed assiduously to God for spiritual discernment, I declare that in my judgment the afore-mentioned apparitions are authentic and are supernatural in character.

I therefore officially approve that the place where they occurred be considered a sacred place. May it become a place of pilgrimage, a place of prayer, reflection and cult; (it is my wish) that liturgical rites be celebrated there, above all the celebration of Mass and the administration of the sacraments of reconciliation and the Eucharist, in accordance with the laws of the Church and the diocesan norms for overall pastoral ministry. (Pastoral Instruction, 21 November 1987, p. 12)

At the conclusion of this same instruction the bishop adds:

I give thanks to God for the privilege of a visit by the Blessed Virgin accorded to our diocese and to our country, because in this period of the history of our Church, marked by a new way of evangelisation, [the visit] invites us to a renewal and deepening of our faith, the living out of our faith in total conversion, prayer and apostolic commitment; because in a divided world Our Lady shows herself as the reconciler of peoples.

May Our Lord grant us that same outpouring of the Spirit which he granted Elizabeth when she was visited by Mary (ibid, p. 22).

This official recognition is a new departure since no apparition had been authenticated for over half a century. This is perhaps due to the fact that the bishop was gifted in respect of discernment, had a good scientific background and was able to harmonise the dictates of a critical approach with the requirements of sound pastoral practice. As God's gardener he cultivated the spiritual fruits of these apparitions. Both he and his flock are the beneficiaries.

Cuapa (Nicaragua) 8 May-13 October 1980

Our Lady appeared at Cuapa to an adult peasant aged about fifty. Bernardo Martinez belonged to a basic Christian community. As at Fatima, Our Lady appeared during a six-month period, from 8 May to 13 October 1980. In all she appeared six times, twice in May (8 and 16 May, on the second occasion to urge him to bear witness, which she had already requested), but not at all in August. There are clear analogies with Fatima: six apparitions in six months from May to October, no apparitions in August and the final apparition on the same date, 13 October.

In the first instance Bernardo saw luminous signs in the chapel (15 April 1980) and then the first apparition on 8 May, during a very trying period of his life. He had no money and was out of work. The maintenance work which he did on the chapel was voluntary and he was considered to be somewhat feeble. He did not know whether he should continue his Christian education in the community. He just wanted to die. After a sleepless night and a more pleasant day fishing in the country, a luminous lady appeared to him at three o'clock, above a pile of stones.

She looked like Our Lady of Fatima. 'She is alive! She is not a statue; she is alive', he said to himself.

He asked her her name.

'Mary', she answered.

'Where do you come from?'

'From heaven; I am the mother of Jesus.'

'What do you want?'

'That you recite the rosary every day.'

'But that is what we already do.'

'I do not want you to recite it only during the month of May, but every day, with your family and with the children as soon as they reach the age of reason. You must say it at a fixed time, as soon as the housework is finished.' She spoke of the situation in the country:

'Nicaragua has suffered terribly since the earthquake and there are more sufferings in store for it. You will continue to suffer unless you change.'

'The Lord has chosen you to pass on this message', she concluded.

It was because he did not dare pass on the message that she appeared to him again during the same month, on 16 May.

'Why did you not pass on what I asked you to say?'

'Because I am afraid. I am afraid of becoming the laughing stock of the people....'

'Do not be afraid. I will help you. Go and speak to the priests.' From then on he spoke out; the apparitions continued on the eighth day of each month. Some believed in them while others ridiculed them.

On 8 September, the Nativity of Our Lady, she appeared as a child as she had to Teresa of Avila and to Bernadette, and she repeated the message of the first apparition (*Le message de la Vierge à Cuapa,* Paris, Éditions Nouveau Service, 1988, p. 48).

Bernardo asked her about the sanctuary which people wanted to erect in her honour. She replied:

'No, the Lord does not want material temples. He wants living temples. You are his temples! Restore the sacred temples of the Lord. It is with you that the Lord is pleased.' Then she added:

'Love one another. Love one another; forgive each other; make peace. It is not enough to ask for peace; make peace.'

Everything is based on faith and love, but charity is a way of life that builds up humanity and the world.

In answer to the question:

'What should be done with the eighty cordobas given by the gentleman from Matagalpa towards building a chapel? Should we return the money?', she replied:

'No. Put them towards the building, but from today do not accept a penny for any purpose' (ibid. p. 48). Bernardo inquired if he should remain in the community.

'Remain on. Little by little you will understand what it all means. You ought to meditate on the beatitudes, away from bustle and noise.'

Finally she added: 'I will not return on 8 October, but on 13 October'; and then the cloud on which she stood rose up as on the other occasions.

Nevertheless Bernardo went back on 8 October as usual, accompanied by a sizeable crowd:

'I knew well she would not come and I had said so. But the people wanted to pray beside the pile of stones where the Virgin appeared' (ibid. p. 49).

At 10.00 on 13 October, after Mass in the chapel, Bernardo went to the place of the apparitions with about fifty people. He saw a luminous ray of light, but it was not until 3.00 in the afternoon that Our Lady appeared to him on the pile of stones which had been covered in flowers. The people insisted that they too should see her. But she wept.

'Why are you weeping?' Bernardo asked.

'It is the hardness of your heart, the hardness of heart of these people which makes me sad. You must pray for them; pray for them so that they might change' (ibid. p. 52).

Then she gave the following message:

'Say the rosary; meditate on the mysteries and listen to the word of God as expressed in these mysteries. Love each other. Pardon each other and make peace. Do not ask for peace unless you make peace. For unless you make peace it is pointless to ask for it.'

The importance and appropriateness of this message for Nicaragua is clear. It is one of the few countries in which peace negotiations, through the help of Our Lady and the intervention of the Pope, have had beneficial results.

She added:

'Fulfil your duties. Put the word of God into practice. Try to be pleasing to God. Help your neighbour. In that way you will be pleasing to God' (ibid. pp. 52-53).

Everybody gave Bernardo a question or a request for Our Lady. He said to her:

'I have a lot of questions and requests, but I have forgotten them.'

'I am asked for things which are unimportant. Ask for faith, so that each of you may have the strength to carry your cross. The sufferings of this world cannot be taken from you. The sufferings are the cross which you must bear.... Do not turn to violence. Never have recourse to violence. Ask for faith so that you may be patient.'

Then she added:

'From now on you will no longer see me in this place.'

'Do not leave me, my mother, do not leave me.'

'Do not worry, I am with you though you do not see me. I am your mother, the mother of all sinners. Love each other. Pardon each other.'

Then once again she emphasised the problems that afflict Nicaragua and the world:

'Make peace; if you do not make peace, then there will be no peace. Do not turn to violence. If you do not change your ways you will provoke the third world war. Pray, pray, my children for the entire world. The world is seriously threatened. A mother does not forget her children. I have not forgotten you, all you who are suffering!'

She concluded as she began:

'I am your mother, mother of all sinners. Invoke me like this: Most holy Virgin, you are my mother, the mother of all sinners.' Then she rose to the top of the branches of the cedar tree and disappeared. This was the final apparition.

According to Bernardo, what is important is the message. 'We are free to accept or reject it. The Lord respects our freedom. I am just a weak vessel through which the message passes. But the Lord makes up for my weakness. We are all very happy that the Lord should have worked this marvel in our midst and we are sure that, provided we observe what we have been told, he will become our Father' (ibid. pp. 54-55).

On 13 November 1983 Mgr P. A. Vega, the sixty-eight-year-old local bishop, caused the following account of the apparition to be published. Though it signifies approval, it is not couched in the legal language of a mandate or a decree of official recognition:

> For the past three years a peasant has been telling of a message which he claims to have received in dreams and apparitions from Mary.... Meanwhile, distorted versions have been disseminated, versions which change the meaning and the content of the message. For this reason, because of my duty to oversee the quality of the piety of the faithful and the truth of the facts, as local bishop, I feel obliged to conserve the authenticity of the facts so that the genuine value of the message may be discerned.... The account which we present adheres faithfully to the content and language of the visionary.
>
> For our part, the emphasis placed on ... the duty to 'make peace and build up the world' is somewhat surprising. The emphasis is not typical of the popular mentality in respect of religion, which would tend to leave everything to God. We present this account as an invitation to reflection on those social obligations which are so often forgotten by a large number of Christians. (Juipalga, 13 November 1983, Pablo Antonio Vega, Bishop Prelate of Juipalga)[2]

This is not a mandate; it is not official recognition of the authenticity of the apparitions. It is simply pastoral advice. The bishop does not say 'The Virgin appears', but rather 'A peasant claims to have received messages either through apparitions or through dreams'. He does not even say 'There are good reasons for believing; I would encourage you to believe.' His desire is to protect the message from 'deformations' and he proposes this message as 'an invitation to reflect' on this social message which merits attention. He remains well within the first phase of the norms laid down by the Congregation for the Faith: the authorisation of existing cults with vigilance, 'so that it bears fruit'.

The bishop saw no need to add anything or to make any changes in this message which, in any case, he feels goes beyond Bernardo's capacity. He invites people to discover its social content for Nicaragua and for the entire world.

Terra Blanca (Mexico)

At Terra Blanca (in the diocese of Queretaro), Elba (thirteen) and Zendia (eleven) claim to see the Virgin, who gives them messages. They write down these messages themselves despite their low level of education. (They now attend a state school run by nuns in Cieneguilla.) Their younger brother also claims to see the Virgin, but he has not written anything. A priest who spent three months at the school attended by the visionaries, and who knows their father, questioned the girls and their brother, methodically and separately. 'Their answers were in agreement', he wrote to me. 'Their descriptions of the Virgin are identical. She gives them time to find paper and a ballpoint pen in order to write the message. They write less frequently since they have come to the Sisters' school (1986/87), because they have less time and the apparition respects their schedule.'

The following is a summary of the message: 'My Son suffers because of the multitude of sins.' The Virgin speaks of the crucifixion, the sufferings of the Passion and the intolerable offences against God which are the cause of these sufferings. We should go to confession; we should pray (particularly the rosary); we should read the Bible and we should fast. In this poor area where people suffer from malnutrition, Our Lady does not request abstention from food, but, rather, from salt. Once, in mid-March 1987, the young brother, Adam, passed on an invitation to fast on bread and water on 25 March and he gave the names of the people who should undertake this. The child did not realise that it was the feast of the Annunciation.

On 15 March 1987 Our Lady gave a very beautiful sign which would appear to be for the local community. She invited them to build a basilica.

On 22 April of that year she said:

> My children, I, your most holy mother, have come to ask for peace and, for that purpose, I speak in many places over the entire world... my children, pray a lot....

This is a somewhat surprising statement, because these little Mexicans from this out-of-the-way corner of the world knew nothing about the rest of the world or about other (current) apparitions.

These apparitions took place in a very poor area, though the spiritual environment was of a very high quality: simplicity, kindness, peace, generosity, prayer etc. Just as in Medjugorje, the visionaries are not at odds with their companions, among whom are to be found other young girls possessing the same virtues.

The children's father states simply how profoundly these apparitions have changed his life of faith. The fruits of the apparitions are striking for this family, isolated in a semi-desert area, for many of the neighbouring families and for the tiny community at the school attended by the children.[3]

San Nicolas[4] (Argentina) since 1983

At San Nicolas (near Buenos Aires) Gladys Quiroga de Mota, a forty-eight-year-old mother, claims to have seen the Virgin since 25 September 1983, at a place known as Campito. The apparition resembles the image of Our Lady of the Rosary which has for some time been venerated in the cathedral. She smiles and becomes sorrowful. The child she holds in her arms does not speak. She recommends prayer and penance.

On 7 October she requested that a sanctuary be built on the spot of the apparitions near the home of the visionary. On 13 October the visionary received a personal message and on 15 November a message for the public.

'I am the patron of this region. Ensure that my rights are honoured. I wish to live beside you. The water is a blessing.'

On 17 November Gladys sprinkled the apparition with holy water as Bernadette had done at Lourdes on 14 February 1858 and Vicka at Medjugorje on 26 June 1981. Once again the Virgin smiled at her and uttered words of encouragement.

On 19 November 1953 she received her mission: 'You will become a bridge of union. Proclaim my words.' And on 22 November: 'Very soon I wish to live beside you.' On 24 November Gladys had a vision of the sanctuary to be built at Campito and the Virgin said: 'I wish to live in this place.'

On 25 November: 'The Holy Spirit is your guide, you must obey. I choose the place where I want to live. Everything is in your hands.' The use of the singular and plural possessive pronoun varies, according to whether the message applies to Gladys alone or to the Church or to all others apart from herself.

On 26 November: 'My desire is to live amongst you, to fill you with blessings, peace and joy and to bring you closer to the Lord our God.'

On 27 November (the first day of the Novena of Saint Nicholas, patron of the town) Gladys found a statue abandoned in the belfry. The Virgin appeared to her and said: 'They had forgotten me but here I am. Place me here. Do not be sad. I will be there very soon. I wish to remain on the banks of the Parana. Remain strong and do not be faint-hearted'.

It was the liturgical feast of the Miraculous Medal during the month of November, the month of flowers and of Mary in the southern hemisphere. The official series of messages (numbered here for the sake of convenience) began on 17 November 1983. It was Jesus who gave the first one to Gladys.

These messages were not recorded (in writing) until after 17 November of that year. The following are the first of these messages:

17 November 1983:
> Rejoice in me, my dear children. Glorious days await you.

The following are the messages from the Blessed Virgin:

28 November 1983:
> He listens to your supplications but you, in your turn should heed his by living as good Christians and listening to his word.... Let him not have suffered Calvary and died in vain. He is risen and wants you to have eternal life. Learn to carry

63

your cross. Accept it as he accepted his. Read Peter's first Epistle, 4:1.2 and 7 up to the end.

1 December 1983:

You will gather what you have sown. It will be the same for what the Lord has ordained. Do not waste time, the night is coming. Use your time while the day is still with you. I want to see you working on my behalf. Glory to God.

On consecration, 7 November 1984:

Ah, my children, I desire strong and faithful hearts, hearts that do not waver and are consecrated to the desire of ascertaining how the Lord will make you live in him.

7 December 1984:

Dearly beloved children, when hearts change as yours have, it is the work of the Lord who has given you the gift of faith. It is up to you to increase this gift because Christ gives his spirit to all those who are consecrated to him. Amen. Amen.

21 September 1986:

May consecration be a binding link between your hearts and mine.

Among the more recent messages:

No. 1175:

It is not the man without bread who is poor, but the man without God.

No. 1185 (30 May 1987):

There are very few who understand the importance of this moment in the history of humanity. This is why I ask my dear sons: live this period of grace; live it to the full and you will not fear the night. Glory to the Lord.

No. 1192 (6 June 1987) — the day on which the Pope recited the rosary on television:

My daughter, at this time there is extreme need for prayer. On this day the Lord will listen to the rosary as if it were my voice. My request, a request to all peoples, is for prayer. Prayer should spring from a heart that is well disposed. It should be frequent and offered with love. Do not neglect prayer for it is the weapon which will overcome the enemy.

No. 1194 (8 June 1987):
My daughter, during this novena all should pray that humankind may experience a hunger for God. If this does not happen humankind will inevitably be lost. There is only one way to be saved—to be nourished by God. Sin and suffering in the world are due to a lack of hope and confidence in God. The world lives in darkness because it does not want the light. Praise be to the most high.

15 September 1987:
Pray, my daughter, that my heartbreak may pass and that I may be consoled.

21 September 1987:
Youth rushes sadly to perdition along the easy road of drugs. This is the panorama which the evil one spreads in front of them: a whole range of sin separates them more and more from God. All that is required is that they look to the mother of God, their mother, and she will lead them to God. They must enter into the mind of Mary in order to hear the voice of God. I do not hide myself. No one should avoid me. Amen. Read Luke 12:29-32.

24 September 1987:
Many are those who, though consecrated, do not abandon themselves to me. They remain deaf to my requests. They do not pray. They lack charity and humility....

25 September 1987, the fourth anniversary of the apparitions:
My dear daughter, I have been with you now for four years. It is in this place that I open my heart. It is from here that I bestow blessings and consolation and it is from this very spot that I offer my son's love to all humanity. I wish to have a dwelling place in this land that God has chosen and from here I will pour out my love on all my children.

27 September 1987:

My daughter, it is Christ who loves, Christ who asks, Christ who waits to change people's hearts for the better. Blessed be the Lord who desires the conversion of his people....

20 October 1987:

I never forget my children and it is from here that they will receive my motherly response. A sanctuary with the living presence of Mary will rise up from this flat countryside. You will not see me, but my heart will tremble with love for my dear children. My children will be gathered into this great building. It will unite and purify my flock.

23 November 1987:

Give me proof of your love, my dear children, by consecrating yourselves to my heart.... Respond to my call and you will see to what tenderness I will lead you. Amen. Amen.

25 November 1987:

On the 25th of each month, my dear children, you come in greater numbers.... My maternal action is having an effect on my children. It is God's grace which is present through his mother. It is the love of God which is made manifest through his mother. It is the mercy of God which is being felt....

5 December 1987:

My dear children, the sweetest drink that can pass your lips is the Word of God. I make it available to all. May souls give themselves to God, abandon themselves to him. May he be praised. Read Isaiah 52:6.

25 January 1988, a day of pilgrimage. Our Lady recalls her life:

On this day of the Annunciation I experienced unparalleled joy. I did not understand and yet my joy allowed me to give my consent.... At Christmas, having spent many hours looking for shelter, we came to the stable, with Joseph, and there on that cold night Jesus was born, in great poverty but protected by my maternal warmth.... My Son filled me with joy from the very moment of the Annunciation and he still fills me with joy by allowing me to be present with him on this day in order to invite souls to conversion.

27 January 1988:

Everything has its season. There is a time for sadness and a time for joy. There is a time when one is estranged and a time when one is found again.

8 February 1988:

My daughter, I am seeking out all my children, the poor and the rich, believers and non-believers. They are all my children. I inherited them at the foot of the cross of Christ. I ask them all to be humble of heart to please Christ. Humility is precious in the eyes of God. Humility allows us to experience our insignificance and to desire to be close to God. Through humility, my dear children, you merit the glory of the Lord. May he be blessed. May all your brothers know how much they are loved by their mother. Read Zephaniah 3:12.

Though the messages of San Nicolas are in general positive and optimistic they also allude to the threats which menace the world because of sin:

Two-thirds of humanity are contaminated *(13 September 1986, No. 966)*. I will cause to perish on earth all things which do not have their origin in heaven *(30 September 1987)*.

Mgr Domenico Salvador Castagna, Bishop of San Nicolas, set up a committee of six priests to examine this phenomenon and the messages. A further team of doctors, psychiatrists and psychologists from the University of Salvador issued a positive report in 1985/86. There are no doctrinal errors in the messages. In Gladys' case there are no signs of hallucinations or pathological states.

The bishop takes charge of the numerous pilgrims (more than 50,000 on the 25th of each month) at a Mass in the cathedral. In the afternoon there is a procession from the cathedral to Campito where Mass is celebrated while confessions are heard.

The bishop has presided over a number of processions. The diocesan curia helps to disseminate the messages throughout the country.

On 25 January 1987 Mgr Castagna preached a homily on the subject of the pedagogy of Our Lady. The bishop also had conversations with the Pope on the subject of the apparitions during the Pope's visit to Argentina in the same year. On returning to Buenos Aires, the Pope requested his pilot to fly over Campito at as low an altitude as possible.

The bishop agreed to the construction of the sanctuary requested by the apparition and the local municipality gave the site of Campito free of charge. Contributions are flowing in from the faithful and the bishop has already laid the foundation stone of the church. The cult, resulting from the apparitions, is firmly under control. It is fruitful. There have been conversions, a renewal of prayer and many cures. In particular, there was the case of a nine-year-old child, cured of a brain tumour. There are also signs in the sun.

Everything would seem to indicate that progress is being made towards an official recognition. Is this possible before the end of the apparitions? Events in Betania (see pp. 53-56) would seem to indicate that it is.

Mgr Castagna has given a good example of the form that pastoral care should take. In a climate of unilateral rejection of apparitions — which tend to be marginalised with consequent divisions, deviations and confusion, the bishop was able positively to channel the graces accorded to his diocese and beyond.

I am not suggesting that every apparition merits being taken over in this manner. In recent years the accepted view was that refusal and suppression were the safer routes. In many cases the refusal caused divisions and deviations that might have been avoided. Where real prayer exists in an atmosphere of fruitful obedience it is often wiser to welcome and guide the crowds which follow. This is perhaps the best policy for the prevention of the digressions inherent in human nature.

Kibeho (Rwanda) 1981-83

The young people
At Kibeho in Rwanda the Virgin appeared to six young people,

three of them boarders in a college run by sisters in a poor area and three living in the bush.[5]

Alphonsine, aged fifteen, was the first to have an apparition, on 28 November 1981. The others followed in their turn. It was not a group apparition; each visionary saw it individually and at irregular intervals. There was no tension or rivalry between the individuals. The apparitions ceased for all the visionaries towards the end of 1983, with the exception of Alphonsine, who continues to experience an apparition on 28 November each year.

I was present at the apparitions on 28 November 1986. The first occurred quietly in the late morning in the girls' dormitory. It lasted almost twenty minutes. The second occurred outdoors at nightfall. A large gathering of Africans was present. It lasted about an hour. Everyone heard what Alphonsine said to the Virgin (there were excellent microphones installed), though only Alphonsine heard the Virgin speak. At the outset of the apparition in the light of the setting sun we could see two big tears running down her cheeks while she repeated: 'So few! So few!'

She explained to me after the apparition: 'The Virgin said to me "I will appear to you only twice more: on 28 November 1988 and on one other occasion"; but she did not give a precise date.'

Segatasha

Independently of the apparitions of Our Lady to the six young people, Christ appeared to a young pagan, Segatasha, to whom he explained who he was and whom he instructed in the faith. Priests were astounded at the soundness of his doctrine in those areas which had been thus revealed to him and, equally, at his appalling ignorance of the rest — though he was extremely eager to assimilate that also. The Lord had given Segatasha a mission of evangelisation which he was pursuing, not without difficulty, in the neighbouring countries. He was expelled from Burundi, but met with success in Zaire in 1986/87, and his current evangelisation in his own country is very fruitful.

Message and results

As at Medjugorje the message is an invitation to prayer and conversion. Fasting is also part of the message. The message has resulted in conversions at all levels and a profound spiritual renewal. There has been a surprising upsurge in vocations (to the priesthood and religious life), not only in the diocese itself, but throughout the country. The message of peace and reconciliation has promoted a climate of brotherhood and mutual aid. On 19 August 1982 the apparition wept and the visionaries wept with her, because she showed them disquieting images of the future: deadly combat, a river of blood, abandoned corpses and a gaping abyss ...

> The world has teeth ... sins are more numerous than drops of water in the sea, the world is rushing headlong to its own destruction (message heard by Anatalie in 1983, G. Maindron, ibid, p. 182).

Segatasha appears to be foretelling the end of the world:

> Too many people treat their neighbours dishonestly... The world is full of hatred. You will know my second coming is at hand when you see the outbreak of religious wars. Then, know that I am on the way (ibid., p. 155).

On 15 August 1988 Mgr Gehanany gave his 'approbation to the public cult of Kibeho, at the site of the apparitions'. Alphonse's last two public apparitions took place at Kibeho on 28 November 1988 and 1989. However, several visionaries still have private apparitions.

Zeitoun (1968)[6] and Shoubra (1986): Cairo (Egypt)

Two series of apparitions took place in the suburbs of Cairo: at Zeitoun from 2 April 1968 to September 1970 and at Shoubra, ongoing since 1983 and more frequent since 1986. Shenouda III, Pope of the Coptic Church, separated from Rome but engaged in positive dialogue with the Holy See, recognised both series of apparitions.

They have two peculiarities in common: Muslims also see them and the apparition allowed itself to be photographed. One of the photographs was published on the front page of an esoteric magazine, *L'Inconnu*, in May 1987 (no. 132):

> At Shoubra, on the night of 10-11 April the commission of inquiry went up to the roof of the Church of St Damian to get a closer view of the apparition. At midnight the bishops of the papal commission arrived, Bishoy, Paulas, Moussa and Moussad. They remained until morning. They heard

the witness of the apparitions and went onto the roof to get a closer view of the phenomenon. They were accompanied by Fr George who was acting on behalf of the parish priest, who was ill. At 3.40 a.m. on Friday 11 April, they all saw the Virgin very clearly surrounded by a halo of dazzling light; the apparition continued until 5.00 a.m.

The commission concluded:

> Let us thank the Lord for this blessing on the people of Egypt and for the repetition of this phenomenon. We would also like to thank the police and the Department of the Interior for their untiring efforts at maintaining safety and good order among the thousands of people who have spent day and night at prayer. We ask all the people to remain calm. Thus they may worthily receive the blessing of the Virgin, of St Damian and of all the saints. May God save our country. We pray that he may guide Egypt and all her children to every success. May this phenomenon be a pledge of well-being for them and for all the nations.

The parish priest, Fr An el Meddia Sherbini, has been restored to good health after the exhaustion of the events surrounding the apparitions. He is assisted by Frs George and Roufail in welcoming the many visitors.

There is one remaining difficulty. There is a photograph of the apparition in circulation, a silhouette of the Virgin, bearing the seal of the Patriarch. This is a poor reproduction of a well-known negative taken at Necedah in the USA during the course of a series of apparitions (1950-52), which were not approved by the local bishop (1955 and 1969); the visionary in that case in fact left the Catholic Church.

Other reproductions of the Necedah negative were circulated as originals taken by a deaf-mute Italian (who has not been identified) at Medjugorje. But the visionaries saw no resemblance to the apparition which they had seen. The oldest negative (Necedah) is a rather good picture in the primitive Italian style. The Virgin is crowned with roses and has an infant in her arms. Enthusiasts believe that these alleged photographs could be used to prove the identity of the person who appears in other apparitions. According to them it represents the real face of Our

Lady. An examination of the photographs would seem to prove that it is an original negative that has been touched up and disimproves from copy to copy, posing serious problems of verification.

I mention this without for a moment denying the beneficial effects of prayer, hope and conversions, and not intending any slight on the evidence of the Coptic commission. While continuing to favour the more rigorous methods adopted in Catholic procedures, I do, of course, respect the oriental method, which is much more direct, less suspicious and more open to the astonishing spontaneity of God's gifts to humanity.

An Egyptian gentleman sent me a photograph taken by his father at the apparitions of Zeitoun in 1968. This photo does not pose any of the problems mentioned above.

Damascus (Syria) since 1982

It all began in November 1982. 'Myrna' (Maria Al Akhras, eighteen) and Nicolas Nazzour (in his thirties) had been married in May. Myrna had put up a small plastic-framed postcard in the courtyard of the large house they shared with the rest of the family. She had bought the cheap mass-produced postcard in Sofia. On 27 November the picture began to exude oil, drop by drop, and filled an alabaster saucer. The phenomenon was repeated.

Some days previously, on 22 November, Myrna's hands began to give off oil as she was praying with a group for Nicolas' sister, Leila, who was ill.

This repeated phenomenon defies reason. Myrna accepts it graciously, simply as an incomprehensible gift connected with anointing, of which it is a sign. Might it also be an image of Our Lady? Scripture teaches us that we are images of God, images of Christ by the anointing of the Holy Spirit. A sign was given at Damascus: sick people asked to be anointed with the miraculous oil and they were cured. Samir Hanna had been paralysed by a stroke followed by a brain haemorrhage. She was cured on 11 December 1982, as was Ghalya Armouche, also of paralysis on 17 December, and many others.

In the face of these phenomena Myrna and Nicolas ask themselves: 'What does the Lord want? Perhaps he is waiting for something?' Myrna prays thus:

My God, what is the meaning of this oil, what is it? No doubt, your divine power. But why have you chosen me in all my weakness, when there are thousands more worthy of this grace than me? Nevertheless, thy will be done. Now I offer you everything—my actions, my chores, my sufferings and my joys — all in your honour, for no other motive. O God, I place all my hope in you. Keep me from anything that would be contrary to your will.

From 15 December onwards the Virgin appeared to Myrna. Three days later, on 18 December 1982, at 11.37 p.m., the apparition gave the following message, which appears to announce a new outpouring of the Spirit:

My children, be mindful of God. God is with us. You know a lot, but you know nothing. Your knowledge is incomplete. The day will come when you will know all things as God knows me. Deal kindly with those who do you wrong; do not mistreat anybody. I have given you oil, more than you have asked. I will give you something stronger than oil. Repent and believe. Be mindful of me in your joy.

There followed a message of evangelisation:

Preach my Son, Emmanuel. Those who preach him are saved. Those who do not preach him are false believers. I do not ask you to give money to churches; what I ask is love. Those who give money to the poor and to the churches and yet have not love, are worthless. I will visit your houses more frequently, because those who go to church do not always go there to pray.

These final phrases seem to predict further apparitions and they seem to be aimed at those whose attendance at Mass is merely an occasion to display their finery.

At the subsequent apparition, Saturday, 8 January 1983, again at 11.37 p.m. (the fourth apparition), the Virgin used only the language of tears. The message of the fifth apparition, Monday, 21 February 1983, 9.30 p.m. was an invitation to humility, not through insulting the proud but rather through forgiveness. She invited them to memorise and repeat these words: 'God saves me, Jesus enlightens me, the Holy Spirit is my life. Therefore, I fear nothing.'

Then there was a call to 'my son, Joseph' which those present did not understand. It touched Fr Malouli to the quick. No one knew that his name was Joseph (he proved it by showing his identity card). This reassuring call was in response to his request for a sign so that he would not commit himself foolishly.

The message of the sixth apparition, Thursday, 24 March 1983, at 9.30 p.m., is one of ecumenism and prayer for this country which is home to so many Christian persuasions:

> The Church is the kingdom of heaven on earth. Those who divided it have sinned and those who rejoice in the division commit sin. Jesus founded it on small beginnings. When it grew divisions also grew. Those responsible for these divisions do not have love. Come together. Pray, pray, pray. How beautiful are my children when they are humbly on their knees. Do not be afraid. I am with you. Do not be divided as grown-ups are. Teach these words to all generations: unity, love and faith.

This message of faith, prayer and confidence is an invitation to conversion which refers to Christ's sadness in the presence of sin and also to the threats that hang over the world—war, famine, unknown sicknesses (which were not revealed). It is also a message of peace set against the divisions and the dividers of the Church, a new invitation to base Christian unity on love.

Myrna received the stigmata on Friday, 25 November 1983 and on two other occasions — on the Thursday and Friday of those years on which Orthodox and Catholic Christians celebrated Easter on the same day: 1984 and 1987. This coincidence will occur only twice before the end of the millennium — in 1992 and in the year 2000.

My visit to Damascus
The following are the notes which I took on the occasion of my visit to Damascus to coincide with the fifth anniversary on 26 November 1987. I arrived the previous afternoon.

> Here I am at Damascus, the town on whose outskirts Paul saw the Lord. This is a live memory here.
> Myrna and Nicolas' house is in the Soufanieh district. It is a house like many others, on the edge of a stream, shaded

by a eucalyptus tree, opposite a mosque. A large Boeing has been transported onto the waste ground in front of the house. It was intended to convert it into a restaurant, but objections from the mosque put an end to that idea. A young family, similar to many others, resides in the house. The husband is an Orthodox Christian, the wife a Greek Catholic.

Nicolas is quite a capable person. Qualified as an up-market ladies hairstylist in Germany, he returned home and, due as much to good fortune as to ability, set up a business operation that left him well-off financially. He reinvested in a high class restaurant at Lattakie on the coast. But he gave it all up as a result of what happened to his wife. He turned over a new leaf and sold the restaurant at a loss.

Myrna is bronzed, smiling and calm. She is bringing up their first child with remarkable care — a lively little girl named Myriam, who was born on 11 October 1986. She is expecting her second child. Who would believe that she has had apparitions and that she has had stigmata on three occasions, like St Francis of Assisi?

The family home has been turned into a sanctuary of sorts. The open courtyard where the picture was set up has been roofed. It has become the central room of the house. Pilgrims file through it calmly, praying before the miraculous image. Fr Malouli collects the oil for the treatment of the sick, who feel better on being anointed. Little Myriam also visits the sanctuary in her push-chair. Under the image there is a handwritten notice in red: 'Sorry, we do not accept gifts or money.' Myrna and Nicolas put the notice there spontaneously without even suspecting that this gesture would prove important to their credibility.

Oil flowed from the image on the night of 26 November. It filled the receptacle beneath it and was discovered later. On the other hand, I was present on two occasions when oil flowed from Myrna's hands. The first was on 25 November, on my arrival, and was unexpected. I went to the Apostolic Nuncio with Myrna, her husband and her little daughter. The child was sleeping on a couch and while we were talking, Nicolas, the husband, whispered to me: 'Look at Myrna's hands.' Oil oozed from them. A nun who was present collected it on swabs of cotton wool as a sign of blessing. Myrna remained calm and simple, the recipient of something she did not understand.

The fifth anniversary
The next day, 26 November, at the vigil of the fifth anniversary of the first apparition, a large crowd packed into the house. It overflowed onto the street. Everyone expected something to happen. I was taken to the couple's room which overlooks the courtyard. It is in this room that Myrna lies down while in ecstasy, during which she is cut off from the outside world.

It all began in darkness. There was a breakdown in the electricity supply (a frequent occurrence in Damascus) shortly before the ecstasy began. Myrna was still standing up. When the light returned we noticed that drops of oil had fallen on the bedspread. Her hands were shining. Those present mopped them up with cotton wool swabs. Myrna came out of the ecstasy after a period of less than an hour. She had been unconscious. One of the doctors, Jamil Margi (a convert from atheism as a result of the events and the cures), who had been following the events closely, did a number of tests. He bent over the bed, examined her eyes, moved her eyeballs energetically. No reaction. He pinched her left forearm hard enough to leave a bruise. Again no reaction. But on coming out of the ecstasy, Myrna immediately rubbed her left arm with her right hand. Her sense of feeling had returned and her arm hurt her a little. But she still could not see. Her vision returned after a few minutes. It was while she was still sightless that she dictated to Fr Malouli the final message from Christ. The substance of the message was as follows:

> Unite my heart to your heart and thus you will save suffering souls, above all those who hate you and speak evil of you. You will obtain glory through this life.

The words allude to a dialogue of 26 November 1985 during which Christ asked:

> 'Do you wish to be crucified or glorified?'
> 'Glorified!', she replied naively, for this young smiling mother had no masochistic streak. The Lord smiled,

she recounted, and asked again:
'For the Creator or for the creature?'
'For the Creator', she replied without hesitation.
'Then glory comes through the crucifixion.'

Myrna knows this full well. Two years earlier (25 November 1983) she had received the stigmata of the Passion. All of this is somewhat puzzling and clashes with the views of the wise, even with those of theologians.

What is the point of the stigmata? This phenomenon, which first occurred in the case of St Francis, was so fervently received by the Church that several popes in the thirteenth century punished preachers who spoke out against it.

For Myrna's friends and neighbours this sign is a powerful reminder of the fact that Christ has suffered for us. It has too often been forgotten. Nor is it merely a fact that belongs to the past, because the sufferings of the Son of God are forever contemporary with his eternal 'I am'. They are mysteriously perennial. They remain present. They invite us to complete in our flesh what is lacking in Christ's afflictions for the sake of his body, the Church (Col 1:24).

Then there is the oil. It is very ordinary oil, exceptionally pure olive oil according to chemical analysis of a sample. The analysts were unaware of the origin of the sample. It is not even a scented oil, just ordinary oil. What is the point? Are your olive trees not sufficient?

The 'sensus fidelium'
The people of God who are open to signs from heaven approved, by and large, the signs at Soufanieh. In earlier times this happened with regard to the miraculous medal and also at Lourdes and Fatima ... just as, earlier still, canonisation was by acclamation.

This spontaneous prayer is helped, followed, guided and oriented by two convinced priests: seventy-one-year-old Fr Malouli, a Lazarist, and Fr Zahlaoui, from Prado. They undertake the task with realistic fervour, each according to his temperament; one more enthusiastic, the other more reflective, tending more to the long-term view.

What do the authorities think?
The episcopal hierarchy, as always, prefers to wait, not to err through haste. The problem is complicated because of the number of Christian denominations represented in this ancient city. There are three patriarchs in residence in Damascus—Orthodox, Syrian and Greek Catholic—as well as several bishops of different rites. I contacted these authorities so they would not hear from elsewhere that I had come as an expert, when in fact my visit was informal and in a private capacity.

The Syrian Patriarch seemed to be personally interested, but because Myrna and Nicolas did not belong to his flock, it was not within his jurisdiction. The Greek Catholic Patriarch, Maximos V, took no interest because of an ecumenical agreement in force in Damascus which allowed that, in the case of a mixed marriage, if the husband was Orthodox then the family came under the jurisdiction of the Orthodox Patriarch.

The latter was briefly interested in the event. The image which had attracted such large crowds was transported with great pomp and ceremony to the Church of the Holy Cross on 9 January 1983. I saw the splendid film of the event. But the image no longer gave forth oil in its new location. The disappointment was bitter. After forty-four days the allegedly miraculous image was ingloriously returned wrapped in a plastic bag. The phenomenon began again.

The ordinary people had theories about this: in the church the image was surrounded by collection boxes. In one of her messages our Lady had said: 'I do not ask that you give money to the churches ... I ask for love.' This is what had inspired Myrna and Nicolas to put up their notice forbidding all offerings.

But the actual reason is perhaps more straightforward. A similar interruption took place in Naju (Korea) in the case of Julia Kim's weeping statue. When the Catholic parish priest brought it to his presbytery to have it examined scientifically, it dried up. When it was brought back on 2 February 1987, tears began to flow again (see pp. 105-108).

Checks
In the complex situation at Damascus where the authorities are unlikely to intervene for some time it may be useful to give an initial summary of what is happening.

Strict scientific checks have been carried out — by outsiders. The police (who, in fact, damaged the image when they were removing it) checked out the walls and the surrounds. Doctors have unanimously concluded that a human body (Myrna's) could not produce oil. Yet no trickery has been discovered. If there had been fraud, then surely the perpetrators would have used scented oil to make the affair look more plausible. Nor would they have refused to accept gifts of money. In fact, indications to the contrary would not have been too subtle. These checks were necessary and should be pursued.

Myrna still resembles those of her friends who were with her during the ecstasy — charming and deep. One of her friends, a young mother, spoke perfect French. Another, a medical doctor, was studying with a view to specialisation. Myrna belongs to that ancient Mediterranean race, steeped in culture and close to life. Her mystical gifts do not interfere with her natural behaviour and they cause no disruption of family life. On the contrary, on 23 November 1983, the Virgin insisted: 'I have not come to divide. Your married life will remain as it is.'

What kind of people were Myrna and her husband before the apparitions? What would be their future? I tried to understand their exceptional candour and their openness.

'Were you a devout person before the apparitions?' I asked.

'Just ordinary.' Her parents who were present confirmed this.

'Did you go to Mass every Sunday?'

'Only from time to time.'

'What is the role of prayer in your life? What time do you pray? In the morning? In the evening?'

'At no particular time, except of course for the rosary and for family prayers.' She also prays while she works. It is clear that for her prayer is a way of life, though she is shy and somewhat ill at ease in explaining this.

'Is your family more united now than before these events?'

'It is about the same — though at a deeper level.'

'Have you received messages concerning the future of the world?'

'The blessed Virgin asked me to keep that matter secret until my death-bed, when I will disclose it.'

Among the messages that have been made known, is that from Our Lord, given to her on 26 November 1985:

'Go to the land where corruption is widespread.' And again on 6 November 1986: 'Let not the things of this world trouble you, because through my wounds you are gaining eternity.'

Again I asked: 'At the outset you saw the Virgin, now you see Christ. How does he appear to you?'

'In a light in which he is a brighter light. I am unable to distinguish his characteristics.'

'Are the stigmata painful?'

'Yes.'

'Worse than the pains of childbirth?'

'The pains of childbirth last longer. The stigmata are more intense.'

'During the stigmata do you see the Passion of Christ?'

'No. I live it, but I do not see it.'

Myrna is an intuitive person. Her experience is deeply felt, but she has difficulty in formulating her answers. She hesitates, smiles, sometimes does not find the words and prefers to remain silent rather than give an irrelevant answer. This is in stark contrast to the crystal clarity of the messages she dictates without any hesitation. This she does immediately after the apparitions, because she forgets them as time passes. The messages are outside her capabilities. She is incapable of producing such maxims.

I also questioned her husband:

'Have these events changed your life?'

'More than one hundred per cent.'

'But in what way?'

'Firstly, my return to the faith, which was very much in the background during my studies in Germany. Then my way of thinking. I used not believe in sin. Now I understand it clearly. I fought. I was vengeful. The messages have taught me to forgive well beyond the point of an eye for an eye ....'

'Has your marriage changed?'

'It has become holy, sacred. When I met Myrna I said, "What is the point of getting married in church? What good will that do?" However, she insisted and so did our families. I agreed because it was the conventional thing to do, but not out of conviction. And when the oil began to flow I asked Myrna not to talk about it, on the grounds that it would make life too complicated. Myrna obeyed me, but she remained puzzled. Then at the subsequent apparition the Virgin said to her, "Do not be afraid, open your doors. Do not deprive anyone who is looking for help.'' '

What Nicolas foresaw was, in fact, what came to pass. Their comfortable family home is full of visitors coming and going. They can no longer call it their own. It has made life difficult: their privacy is gone, their work hampered and even their rest is interrupted.

At that time the 'Muslim Brotherhood' was on the rampage. There was the danger of reprisal from that quarter and also from the Churches because of their mixed marriage. They embarked on this unusual adventure with calm self-denial. Nicolas' mother spends her time cleaning the courtyard so that it may be worthy of Our Lady.

The house itself is being altered constantly in order to adapt it to the new needs. The barrier of the balcony has been raised and reinforced, as it was in danger of collapsing under pressure from the crowds. I asked Nicolas: 'Are you happier now than you were before?' 'We have lost financially. But in my heart of hearts I am happier. We have lost the earth but gained heaven.'

Fruits

Above and beyond the scientific investigations and the police inspections we are invited by the gospel to judge these events according to the simple criterion: 'A tree is judged by its fruit.' In Myrna's family and among the many visitors, the fruit is remarkable.

This is the substance of the message given to Myrna during an ecstasy on Ascension Thursday, 31 May 1984:

> My daughter, I am the Beginning and the End. I am the truth, freedom and peace. My peace I give you.[7] Those who do not seek the approval of the crowds and who are not afraid of disapproval, will receive real peace, which is fulfilled in me. Live your life quietly and independently. May the burdens which you bear for me not break you. Rejoice, I will be your recompense. Your trials will not continue and your sufferings will not last. Pray. Adore. Eternal life is worth these sufferings. Pray that the will of God may be fulfilled in you and say:

> Dearly beloved Jesus,
> Grant that I may find rest in you
> above all things,
> above every creature,
> above all the angels,
> above all praise,
> above all joy and exultation,
> above all glory and honour
> above all the heavenly army.
> Because you alone are the Most High.
> You alone are powerful and good beyond all.
> Come to me and console me.
> Loose my chains.
> Give me freedom.
> Because without you my joy is incomplete.
> Without you my table is bare.
> Then I shall come and say to you:
> Here I am. I come because you have invited me.

In March 1988 Myrna and Nicolas were invited to the USA for six months by one of Mr Reagan's doctors, Dr Mansou of Los Angeles, to spread their message. Nicolas' mother continues to welcome visitors and to clean the courtyard where the little image of Our Lady still hangs.

Medjugorje (Yugoslavia): ongoing since 24 June 1981

On 24 June 1981, six young Croatians saw a silhouette on the hill of Crnica near the Franciscan parish of Medjugorje in the Croatian region of Hercegovina. They were at the foot of the hill (Podbrdo) but they did not dare climb up. On the following day four of the original group returned — Mirjana, Ivanka, Ivan and Vicka. Ivan Ivankovič and Milka Pavlovič were absent but they were replaced by Milka's sister, Maria Pavlovič and ten-year-old Jakov. The others were aged between fifteen and sixteen. On the second day they climbed the hill, saw the Virgin close up and began to converse with her. Since then, the *Gospa* (Croatian for Our Lady) appears to them every day: she is young, clothed in a bright, silver-grey garment, and has wavy black hair beneath a white veil. Around her head there is a circle of twelve stars. Her eyes are blue. She looks at them with extraordinary affection.

From 25 to 29 June the apparitions took place on the hill of Crnica which overlooks the hamlet where the visionaries live (Biakovici). However the police soon made the hill out of bounds.

From 30 June the apparitions took place secretly in order to avoid the police, and gradually the church became the location. They occurred between the rosary and Mass in the presence of huge crowds of parishioners and pilgrims. To shield them from the curious, the visionaries were moved to a small adjoining changing-room cum sacristy which thus became the 'chapel of the apparitions'.

Initially the local bishop was favourably disposed. However, for reasons of local politics and, in particular, an ongoing row between himself and the Franciscans, he forbade the visionaries to use any premises adjoining the church. For this reason they transferred to the local presbytery. The move was somewhat to the detriment of the liturgical coherence of the event. In August 1987 the presbytery was also forbidden as a location by the bishop. Again a solution was difficult to find. Since then the apparitions take place in a more discreet fashion — in the home of each visionary or, if the visionaries are in the church for Mass, behind locked doors on the gallery with no witnesses.

Two of the first group of visionaries no longer see the apparition, having received the tenth and final secret from Our Lady — Mirjana at Christmas 1982 and Ivanka on 7 May 1985. The Virgin promised them an apparition once a year — on her birthday (18 March) for Mirjana and on the anniversary of the first apparition (25 June) for Ivanka.

The substance of the message was given on the first five days. It recalls the essence and urgency of the gospel: return to God through conversion, faith, prayer and fasting. Through these practices a divided world will gain peace and reconciliation.

This message is followed closely in the parish. There is no other parish in the world where so much prayer takes place. It is marked by crowded daily masses, personal prayer, recitations of the rosary and bread and water fasts every Wednesday and Friday. Many prayer groups have emerged which contribute to the building up of the faith.

Some of the reconciliations have been spectacular. The parish had been divided and in the 1940s violent quarrels between the hamlets of Biakovici and Medjugorje had led to armed fighting and deaths. 'Now we are all brothers', say these former enemies.

There are ten well-kept secrets regarding the destiny of the world. They will be revealed in due course, three days before each of them is fulfilled. The visionaries would have us understand that many of the secrets have to do with the threats hanging over the world, abandoned to sin and preparing its own destruction.

The 'secret' messages are somewhat problematic. They may well prove a disappointment because even the saints were mistaken in matters of prediction. It would be imprudent to accept these 'secrets' as gospel.

As regards the essence of the events, after seven years I, as an expert, am convinced. The fruits of holiness are admirable among the visionaries whose growth in spirituality is astounding and has not diminished their natural simplicity; in the parish and surrounding area where so many prayer groups and vocation circles have sprung up, among pilgrims where conversions multiply and in the dozens of confessors who are in attendance every day — on 25 June 1988 there were 150.

Added to this is the evidence of medical tests which excludes all traces of the pathological. Then there are cures. In all some 330 have been recorded since 1981, some of which have been remarkable. Two have been confirmed after investigations that would have done more than justice to similar tests carried out at Lourdes.

Damir Corič (born 23 July 1960) had contracted internal hydrocephalis with subdural haematoma. He had been operated on five times since 1980; meanwhile he had become bedridden, was unable to walk, speak or eat and had lost control of his bowel movements. In July 1981, after Vicka had prayed for him, he regained his speech, was again able to walk and regained perfect health. In October 1983 he went back to work in a compressor factory in Mostar. The medical examination which he underwent on that occasion found that he was perfectly fit for work. However, tests made in 1980 still bear witness to noticeable deterioration of part of the brain.

The other cure was that of Diana Basile. She had been suffering from multiple sclerosis since 1972. She was blind in her right eye, had difficulty in moving her arms and legs and suffered from urinary incontinence. She felt a great sense of interior warmth as she entered the little chapel of the apparitions for the visionaries' ecstasy. Her whole life passed before her as in a film. She was cured. The next day she walked the ten kilometres from her hotel to Medjugorje and, barefoot, climbed the steep hill of the apparitions.

Finally, in April 1987 the bishop came to Rome to present the draft of his negative judgment. However, Cardinal Ratzinger requested him to dissolve his commission of inquiry. The Cardinal took the matter out of his hands and handed over responsibility to the Yugoslav episcopal conference. I have no intention of anticipating the outcome; in any case a definitive judgment cannot be made until the apparitions have ceased.

One thing, however, did impress me deeply. When opposition was at its greatest, coming as it did from the police, the government and the bishop simultaneously, when the place was thronged with crowds and there were no facilities for their reception, I believed that all was lost and that in those impossible conditions the only outcome could have been illuminism, disillusionment, revolt or despair. But when the situation was at its worst (during the years 1984 to 1986) the difficulties served only to increase priests', visionaries' and parishioners' devotion to prayer in which they found solutions. This is one of the pillars of my conviction as an expert.[8]

Escorial (Spain): since 1980

Since 13 November 1980 it has been said that the Virgin appears to Amparo Cuevas. She is a poor woman, born on 13 March 1931, the mother of seven children, and lives in Escorial, the city of the royal palace, about fifty kilometres from Madrid. Crowds gather there.

I will not dwell on the matter mainly because the archbishop issued a statement on 12 April 1985 to the effect that the supernatural character of the presumed apparitions and messages has not been established. But he does not say that their non-supernatural character has been established. As a matter of prudence he has requested priests to refrain from attending these religious manifestations (the classical attitude which, however, is not without its own risks since it deprives these gatherings of all pastoral guidance and control). My only personal knowledge of current gatherings is from tape recordings, on which the rosary is recited with calm dignity.

What has impressed me is the human and spiritual quality of this visionary who, since childhood, has been subjected to deprivations which could have unbalanced or even destroyed her.

I met her in 1985 in Escorial in the house where she works as a domestic. Her husband does not work and she has had to do the virtually impossible to rear her seven children. She remains simple, calm and natural; there are no signs of over-enthusiasm, pretentiousness or sentimentality. In spite of her poverty, her dress is modest, clean and cared-for. She is not embarrassed by difficult questions and answers each question briefly as it is put to her.

Amparo Cuevas never knew her mother who died when she was just six months old. Her stepmother sent her to sell objects on the street and ordered her to remain there until she had sold everything. The child frequently slept under a tree, having eaten nothing. In winter she sometimes slept covered in snow. On one occasion at the age of nine she had to be resuscitated. At home she had no bed and slept in a cupboard too small to allow her to stretch herself. At the age of ten she was locked up for begging for food in the village and survived on the flour and water diet passed into her cell. She loved the Blessed Virgin and told her in all innocence of her desire to die. 'Dear mother in heaven, I would like to see my own mother. Take me where she is.'

She was convinced that the Blessed Virgin listened to her. Her unhappy childhood was followed by an unhappy marriage. Her idle, alcoholic husband assured the continuation of her martyrdom. At the end of all of this it is surprising that Amparo has retained such dignity and calm, such simplicity and balance. This in itself is evidence that should command our respect. It would lead us to wish that the holiness of the poor be better understood in the Church. From a gospel point of view it appears to me that it is difficult to view this person from the outside, from above. I got the impression that I had seen her from within.[9]

The 'Virgin' has asked that a chapel be built but, above all, she has urgently called for conversion, a return to prayer, to the daily recitation of the rosary. The world, she says, is on the edge of a precipice: unemployment, misery and wars, with signs in the stars.

Amparo received the stigmata so that one third of humanity might be saved from a cataclysm without precedent.

She has succeeded in educating her children, the eldest of whom is now a doctor. Her husband, who never worked and used to drink too much has made a very sincere conversion.

Notes

1. The first account of these apparitions was given by a Spanish priest who visited Finca Betania twice: Agueda Maria Rodriguez, *Estudios Marianos* 52, 1987 (pp. 371-374). The bishop wrote to him on 5 February 1987: 'I am continuing my inquiries with a view to receiving the Pope's recognition of the apparition.'
   Mgr P.B. Ricardo wrote to me from Los Teques (7 April 1988), and attached documentation of his enquiries and his judgment as printed in his Pastoral Instruction.
2. *Le message de la Vierge à Cuapa (Nicaragua), Le témoignage de Bernardo.* Preface by Mgr A. Vega, Éd. Renouveau Service BP 316, 75265 Paris Cedex 06, 1987, 68p.
3. This is based on information provided by a gifted priest who lived for several months in the region and who, because of his interest in the apparitions, returned there. The bishop has remained discreetly silent. The nuns are favourably disposed towards the apparitions and ensure that the children remain humble and discreet. The sisters appreciate the fruit of this special grace.
4. *Mensajes* (1983-85) San Nicolas (Argentina), 1985, 236p. Félix O. Carreras, *Maria de San Nicolas,* Buenos Aires, Éd. Esquiu, 1987, 128p. Also the abundant documentation sent to me from the Bishop's palace (San Nicolas) and by Hélène Gall, whom I thank.
5. Gabriel Maindron, *Des Apparitions à Kibého: annonce de Marie au coeur de l'Afrique,* Paris, OEil, 1984, 248p.
6. M. Niel, *Les Apparitions de la Très Sainte Vierge en Égypte en 1968-1969,* Paris, Téqui, 1980 and J. G. Giamberardini: *Il culto Mariano in Egitto,* Jerusalem, Franciscan Press, 1978, Vol 3, pp. 425-438 (with bibliography and official documents).
7. These sentiments recall key gospel phrases on Christ: Revelation 1:8; John 14:6; John 8:36 (on freedom); Ep 2:14; John 14:27. For more information on the apparitions at Damascus see Christian Rayaz, *Soufanieh, Les apparitions à Damas,* Paris, Mambre, 1988, 164 p.
8. René Laurentin, *La Vierge apparaît-elle à Medjugorje?,* Paris, OEil, 1984 (first overall study); *Apparitions de Marie à Medjugorje; Où est la vérité?,* ibid, *Dernières nouvelles sur Medjugorje,* 7 volumes which from time to time give news of Medjugorje: Medjugorje recit (ibid); *Messages et pédagogie des apparitions de Medjugorje,* with a chronological listing of the messages (ibid) in collaboration with René Lejeune; *Études medicales et scientifiques sur Medjugorje* (Medical and Scientific Studies on the Apparitions at Medjugorje, English translation published by Veritas), in collaboration with Professor Henri Joyeux; Dr M. Margnelli and G. Gagllardi, *Le apparizioni della Madonna* in *Riza-Scienze,* no. 16, July 1987, pp. 14-41: tests and favourable conclusions.
9. *Apparitions et messages de l'Escorial* (Spain), 1983, Beaupréau; *L'Impartial,* 1983 and various works in Spanish.

2

INQUIRY FROM 4 OCTOBER TO 7 OCTOBER 1987

I had come to a first draft of my conclusions. But further information continued to reach me. Before leaving for the Philippines I decided to go to Italy where there had been much talk of apparitions since the beginning of October 1987.

I had expected to find a very questionable situation. Instead I discovered, and to a degree which I had not foreseen, very convincing results and very worthy people people who were, indeed, underestimated. In fact, what I` discovered held my attention without prejudging any ulterior evolution of the situation and without anticipating the judgment of the Church. The following are the notes I took.

Oliveto Citra: since 24 May 1985

Oliveto Citra, like many other small Italian villages, is built on a hilltop. It is about a two-hour drive to the south-east of Naples and has grown into a commercial centre of about 4,000 inhabitants.

At about 10.00 p.m. on 24 May 1985, the feast of St Macario, the patron of the village, twelve children between the ages of eight and ten were playing in the little square in front of Rufolo's pharmacy under the medieval castle. Musical celebrations for the feast day were in full swing in the nearby Piazza Garibaldi.

Suddenly they saw a streak of light in the heavens coming from the direction of the castle 'like a falling star'. They thought of creatures from space but nevertheless they approached the spot and saw a beautiful lady with a child in her arms. She smiled at them. They were at once captivated and troubled. A young man brought them into a bar close by where they were given something to drink to revive them.

Then other children came on the scene and began to shout that they had seen the Madonna. The manager of the bar informed the twenty-year-old waitress of this. Anita shrugged her shoulders but out of sheer curiosity went outside and she, too, saw the Madonna. The apparition said to her: 'You will always see me at night'. She was shaken by the ecstasy. She was taken to the hospital where the doctor on duty, Giuseppe Santini, examined her briefly and concluded that she was healthy in mind and body, but had a certain muscular rigidity as if she had experienced a great shock.

On the following night (25 May) Anita again experienced the apparition at her own home. She asked why she had been chosen: 'It is not you alone that I have chosen. Many will see me but only those who have the courage to believe will remain.'

Anita was to have thirty apparitions and she received messages concerning prayer, penance and fasting. But her father put an end to her visits to the castle.

Meanwhile the rumour spread that on 20 July the Madonna would give a sign. On that day about 2,000 pilgrims gathered in Piazza Garibaldi and in the smaller square in front of the castle. It was 11.00 p.m. The visionaries announced that everyone would see and very soon they saw a luminous red cloud and the message: 'I am sending this cloud as a first sign'. The cloud is said to have been seen from a distance of ten kilometres and fifty witnesses claim to have seen the Madonna.

On 5 August Anita had another apparition during which the Madonna said: 'Today is a feast day, it is my birthday'. This coincides with what happened at Medjugorje where some of the visionaries were invited to celebrate the second millennium of Our Lady's birthday.

On a June evening Dr Luigi Mirto asked Sabrina, another of the visionaries, to put three questions to the apparition in German (a language not understood by any of those present). These are the three questions and the answers to them:

1. Are you the mother of all?
    Yes.
2. What messages would you like us to give humanity?
    Pray, pray, pray.
3. What age are you?
No answer.

There is great surprise at the proliferation of apparitions and of other mysterious phenomena: lights, sweet odours and cures. (Faricy-Pecorcao, pp. 100-110) In response to another question from the visionaries, the apparition answered: 'I am the Madonna of the castle'.

The Apparitions of Our Lady

The following are some of the messages:

2 November 1985 (message to Mafalda Mattia):
> The world is at the edge of a yawning precipice; pray, pray particularly for the heads of the great nations because, being preoccupied with preparing for war and spreading violence, they have no time to pray.

There followed a message which the parish priest was asked to transmit:

> Tell the pilgrims that I am here even though they may not see me; let them come to visit me and ask of me all the graces which they desire.

3 December 1985 (message to Elsa di Rosa, from Ercolano near Naples):
> I have come to bring peace, harmony and joy. (Then three stars appeared.) This is my present to you.

8 December 1985 (message to Rita Rocco from Belizzi, Salerno):
> My wish is that the rosary be recited in the family. I would like to hold you all in my arms.

9 December 1985 (message to Giovanni di Marco from Acropoli, Salerno):
> Pray, pray (...) because the Son of God is tired of people and their sinful ways.

15 December 1985 (message to Tarcisio di Biasi from Oliveto Citra, Salerno):
> You should say to the pilgrims that I do not need flowers and candles. Let them pray, for the time remaining before the chastisements is short.

17 December 1985 (message to Fusco Adriana from Battipaglia, Salerno):
> Humanity's faith has been shipwrecked. They do not have the courage to do what is right. I have come to help you be converted and return to God; that means a return to faith in God, to works of charity and to fervent attendance at Mass.

10 January 1986 (message to Mafalda Mattia):

My dear children, God has sent me down to earth to save you all because the entire world is in danger. I came into your midst to bring peace to your hearts. He wants peace to reign in the hearts of all and he desires the conversion of all. For this object, my dear children, pray, pray, pray. If you do not pray you will receive nothing. The time at your disposal is short. There will be earthquakes and great misfortunes and famine for all the inhabitants of the earth. My dear children, when God comes among you he does not come for amusement. He is not afraid of the powerful nor of the indifferent. So, take this message seriously. I will ask God not to punish you. God says: save yourselves, pray a great deal and do penance.... Humanity is replete with serious sins that are an offence to the love of God. Peace on earth is about to end. The world cannot be saved without peace, but it will find peace only if humanity returns to God.

On 12 January 1986, Tarcisio di Biasi received the following comforting message:

Tell the pilgrims not to be afraid, rather to believe in my son, to do penance and to pray.

On 17 January to the same person:

Because of sins there will be severe chastisements but they can be avoided by prayer and penance.

Similarly, on 28 January 1986 to Agorini Santa of Fratta Maggiore, Naples:

If you pray I will help you escape the plagues which will come upon the earth because of its sinfulness. Many children and young people will see me.

On the road home Agorini Santa saw the Madonna again beside the castle and she said to her:

I would like to embrace you and all of you. Good-bye!

1 February 1986, to Tarcisio:

Dear son, I am so happy that you are praying together. *(And then he heard this intercession):* My son, see how many people are praying, have pity on them!

3 February 1986 to Giovanni di Marco:
> God has accepted community prayer and has promised to ease the chastisements provided prayer and penance continue.

8 February 1986 to Fasona Anna:
> Yes, there will be peace in the world if all are converted and pray a great deal.

My meeting with Antonella

During the early months of the apparitions I had already been contacted by Fr Robert Faricy, SJ, a professor at the Gregorian University in Rome, and by Luciana Pecoraio. The latter went each weekend to Oliveto Citra to help the visionaries in their life of prayer and in their spiritual formation. The concentration on prayer had succeeded in whittling down the number of so-called visionaries. Deep and continuous contact with God had helped to confirm the real visionaries and at the same time brought the others to a more realistic, humble and prayerful realisation of their situation. 'How do you do it?', I asked Luciana, 'How do you separate the real visionaries from the others? Do you question them? Do you challenge them?'

'Nothing of the kind, that happens all by itself through prayer.'

On 3 and 4 October she brought one of the visionaries to Rome to meet me. I was rather sceptical. Doctors Gagliardi and Margnelli were aware of the false sense of excitement and on examining a number of the visionaries had indicated the presence of a chain reaction which had induced the visions.

Antonella, a fifteen-year-old, rather small brunette, was born on 5 August 1973. She is a perfectly simple girl, neither timid nor impudent. She answers questions briefly and to the point and, like Bernadette, never goes beyond the point of the question. When she does not know the answer she says nothing.

She comes from a poor family. For this reason she left school at the age of fourteen and began work as a waitress in the restaurant of her village which is about twelve kilometres from Oliveto Citra. She truly lives a life of deep and calm prayer. When I asked her: 'When you are serving in the restaurant are you able to pray?', she replied, very simply, 'Yes', a little surprised at the question. And I was equally surprised by the answer.

'No doubt when things are quiet, but what about the busy times?

'Yes', she replied, again showing a little surprise.

'Do you see the apparition every day?'

'Every time I go to Oliveto Citra'.

'How often is that?' She is a little slow to give a precise answer and Luciana comes to her aid:

'Antonella's house is twelve kilometres away. It is a very rough road. She does not always have the time to go there on foot and she is not strong enough to do the journey on a bicycle. In fact she goes there as often as she can find someone to give her a lift.... I take her there every weekend.'

There are many apparitions, perhaps too many, at Oliveto Citra, including those had by pilgrims. Doctors Gagliardi and Margnelli have examined a number of them. They have pointed out that in many cases there are no physiological symptoms of ecstasy. No doubt there is some contagion but this seems to be on the decrease. The parish priest, Giuseppe Amato, known as Don Peppino, the vicar general and ordinary of the ancient diocese of Campagna which is now attached to Salerno, is a brave and solid man. He has promoted an atmosphere of prayer. Some might be inclined to the view that his outlook is not sufficiently critical; but he deals with what is most urgent, which is not to be critical but rather to guide people to the Lord with all the means at his disposal as a priest. Without too much intervention on his part things are beginning to be sorted out through prayer. What impresses him are the fruits—conversions, a rise in the level of religious practice and in the spiritual tenor of the parish.

Every evening groups of pilgrims gather for prayer on the piazza in front of the castle. There are conversions and cures. The parish priest is in favour of the apparitions.

A statue of the Queen of the Castle was blessed and inaugurated on 25 April 1987. On 4 August 1986 Mgr Grimaldi, the Bishop of Salerno, had authorised the construction of a small shrine to the Virgin. 'I accept it', he noted, 'as an initiative coming from a private group of the faithful without in any way involving the authority of the Church'. He retains an attitude of very cautious expectancy.

I was in Oliveto Citra on 23 and 24 May 1988. I was able to see at first hand the high quality of the pastoral work carried out by Mgr Giuseppe Amato. This expansive religious phenomenon could easily have deviated. He has tended it carefully, much to the benefit of the parish and the region.[1]

A prayer movement at Schio since 25 March 1985
I visited Renato Baron twice (24 May 1986 and 6 October 1987) in Schio in the diocese of Vicenza. He is in his early fifties and has been married since 1958. He was a local councillor from 1960 to 1985 and has acted as a public assessor in his village from 1970 to 1975. He works as a ticket salesman for the motorway company and plans to take early retirement when he reaches fifty-five. The large centre of prayer and hospitality for the poor which he has founded near his home would be more than enough to keep him busy full-time.

The beginning
On the Feast of the Annunciation in 1985 Renato Baron went to visit the chapel of the Virgin which he maintained on the hillside near his home. He was reciting the rosary, seated on the front bench facing a beautiful coloured statue of the Madonna and Child:

'Before finishing the second Ave I felt as if my mind and body had vanished. All I could see was the statue. It seemed to come to life, it smiled and spoke to me.'

'Come here every day and write down what I tell you,' he heard. He was confused. He did not dare to speak about this strange occurrence, not even to his wife, despite the very close relationship he had with her. Was it an apparition? One would be more inclined to see it as the animation, the transfiguration of this statue before which he prayed and whose sanctuary he maintained. The point is not without importance.

The Virgin revealed herself to him as the Queen of Love[2] and gave him frequent messages. From 3 April 1985 onwards he noted them down on the spot:

> Pray and make sacrifices because it is only through prayer that men will be saved. Even those who go to church are not strong enough in their faith. This is why I have intervened, to do the will of the Father. Turn again towards the Father for he can do all things. The world is heading for perdition.

But in the second message, which took place on 7 April, love is the dominant theme:

> Love the Father with all your heart. Make him be loved. He loves you, listen to his word and to his teachings.

There were nine messages in the course of the month of April. The shortest came on 18 April:

> I am the abandoned mother.

The following is the final one of the month (24 April):

> The Father's immense love will save you. You must personally thank him for everything. He is infinite love. You should also love each other with that same love.

There were two messages in May, six in June, one in July, one in August, eight in September, four in October, eight in November, sixteen in December, and so the pattern continues:

> I will prepare friends for you, apostles, and you will accomplish all things with them. Together we will convert many souls and lead them to Jesus.

This message gave him great confidence and joy. The promises are beginning to be fulfilled. Crowds come to pray. Priests bring along their parishioners and the fruits are durable. People come from the city: a pharmacist, a doctor, a student of economics, who was finishing his thesis, and many others, have returned to prayer and put themselves at the service of the new centre.

My first visit

On the occasion of my first visit to Renato's tiny house on the hillside on 24 May 1986 there were twelve people there. That caused some complaints: 'He thinks he is Jesus Christ with his twelve apostles!', they said. But Renato is simple and modest, a no-nonsense realist. He is a servant of Our Lady. Crowds continue to come and although he would like to restrict the founding group to a smaller number, there are now twenty-six of them.

During this first visit Renato seemed to indicate that the Virgin wanted a modification in the wording of the Hail Mary 'the fruit of your heart' to replace 'the fruit of your womb'. I expressed concern on this point: 'If you want to change the prayer formulas you will have the whole world on your back.'

My second visit

On Tuesday 6 October I again spoke to Renato about this matter. He smiled as if remembering his earlier naivety. It had become a thing of the past: 'We sometimes use this formula when we are among ourselves, but only in private.'

Crowds continue to flow into Schio whether there is an apparition or not. On 6 October the chapel, which is scarcely large enough to hold 100 people, was full to overflowing. With the help of his twenty-six companions, among whom was to be found a wide range of skills and talents, Renato succeeded in finding a five hectare site near his own home, with a beautiful view from the side of the hill. The land, owned by a widow since the death of her husband during the 1960s, was disused. They had no difficulty in finding the necessary money and she handed it over to them.

The twenty-six associate founders repaired the dilapidated house and transformed it into a school for prayer. On the ground floor there is a chapel which is always full. There are two intertwining paths on the side of the hill on which there are the fifteen mysteries of the rosary and the fourteen stations of the cross. Thursday is the day on which they fast. Many come willingly. They enjoy meeting the sporting personality Toto, once one of the idols of Italian football. He is now over thirty and no longer at his peak but nevertheless continues to play as a professional centre-forward with a regional team. He prays with the crowds and his testimony is convincing.

There is an all-night prayer vigil held each Friday night. After cautious deliberation the Bishop has established a commission to draw up a judgment on the case, the fifth session of which was held in November 1987. There is no point in trying to predict the outcome of the commission's deliberations. The fruits of prayer, conversions and cures cannot, however, be disputed. Local parish priests bring their parishioners to Schio, and their own churches, which at times were rather sparsely populated, are now full for Sunday Mass. The influence of the centre is widespread, particularly in the north, from Trieste to Milan; but it also goes beyond that and is felt as far away as Sardinia.

The message

Renato radiates messages of prayer, confidence, love and evangelisation. He is welcomed with joy, simplicity and confidence: prayer can solve everything. As the apparitions said:

> I appear in all parts of the world, to change the world, to take away the sin through which men are preparing the destruction of the world.

'Might this be an announcement of the end of the world?' I asked Renato Baron. He replied 'It is rather the end of a world which men are constructing.' All is centred on the Father: goodness and love the source of all things.

Incidents

I was struck by the warmth of the welcome, the fraternal atmosphere, the calm, serenity and simplicity which prevailed. Everything works out for the best, without apparent effort; they help each other, they are creative, they improvise with that marvellous Italian flexibility. But life is not without incident. The group overcame many trials and obstacles. They were on the look-out for a priest to guide them and their desire for spiritual guidance seemed to be fulfilled in the person of the rector of the Basilica of San Lorenzo in Vincenza. However, it transpired that this priest had certain contacts with a visionary who was somewhat suspect. The bishop asked him to sever the relationship but instead he resigned his post. Then the bishop requested Renato and his companions to break their relationship with the priest. They complied, and asked the bishop, as a matter of urgency, to give them a replacement who would educate and advise them and act as their confessor. There seemed to be a problem. When the commission was consulted they hesitated. To assign them a priest would appear to give recognition to the place even before they (the commission) had completed their work.

This idea is widespread among commissions of inquiry charged with investigating apparitions. It is as though one should work from the outside and not from within as an observer/participant (for fear of being influenced or contaminated). Visionaries should be put to the test rather than helped. If the apparitions prove to be true then the evidence will be all the more manifest; if they are false they will be uncovered more readily. This kind of reasoning is not altogether clear. Visionaries may well be fragile persons needing help and enlightenment and one should pay more attention to the saying *corruptio optimi pessima* (the corruption of the best yields the worst results).

At Schio the bishop went beyond this advice and found a compromise solution: the archpriest of nearby Sant'Orce, a very busy man who is not a member of the commission, comes when he can to minister to the spiritual hunger and thirst of the members of the centre.

More recently there was a different kind of alert. Visitors were caught in the act of vandalising the Way of the Cross. Those who were close by gave chase and the vandals ran off. The associate founders are no weaklings. A show of strength was enough: they did not need to use it. To their surprise the wooden cross which had been damaged began to give off a mysterious perfume. They have installed it in the chapel protected by a perforated rigid plastic surround, through which one can smell the sweet, penetrating, indefinable scent, a combination of incense, flowers and the odour of fruit. Doctor Margnelli has been consulted on the matter.

All this may seem astonishing but it is not today or yesterday that God began to speak to simple people, not in the language of the wise, but in simple language, that of perfume and flowers and even of tears. One might be tempted to say that this is pietism, dreaming, prayer gone wild, forgetful of commitment and service. But then Renato Baron has been invited not only to prayer but also to provide hospitality for the most abandoned, the poor, the sick and even the mentally handicapped. The twenty-six have already drawn up plans for the construction of a large house devoted to such hospitality.

Little R

During this same visit to Italy I twice had an opportunity to meet an eleven-year-old girl who has experienced ecstasy every day since 20 March 1987.

'Do you wish to praise the Lord with me?', the apparition said to her.

'Yes, Mama from heaven, I do.'

'Praised be Jesus Christ.'

'Always.'

Her parish priest wanted me to meet her. He is a brave and solid man who has emphasised the importance of prayer in his parish. He is in obedient contact with his bishop who has instructed him to remain cautious. For this reason I give neither the girl's name nor the name of the locality, though some Italian newspapers have spoken about the event.

R is a small blonde girl. Academically she is not very gifted; she is in the bottom half of her class. She quickly forgets the messages. For this reason she notes them down immediately after each apparition. She writes in capital letters for the sake of clarity and so that it will be more worthy of Our Lady. There are about ten lines in each message. I once witnessed her writing while resting on the edge of a dresser in such an uncomfortable position that I found a table for her. She has two sisters and one brother. Her parents, who were not practising Catholics before this event, now keep fervently and closely in touch with her.

This is important for the little girl who often suffers for hours at a time. The Virgin had warned her that she would suffer. This is her share in the Passion of Christ and she accepts it.

But she lives in the present. When she is asked about one of the messages she can never recall it immediately. Then when it is read back to her she exclaims with joy: 'How beautiful!'

She converses in extremely familiar terms with Our Lady; it is like the chatter of a child with her mother. She writes the messages rapidly in the script of a child. On 2 October 1987 she noted the following dialogue with Mary:

'Fr M asked me to thank you for all you have done.'

'I have done nothing', replied the Virgin.

'What do you mean?' exclaimed R, taken aback.

'It is God who has done everything!'

'You could have told me this sooner.'

'My dear children, today I invite you all to become saints.'

'But this is very hard, Mama.'

'Well I have been able to do it, so too can you.'

'But you are the queen of saints.'

'I am not asking you to become kings.'

'All right, Mama, we understand your hurry.'

R notes that at this point the Virgin smiled and then carried on with the reply:

'I am in a hurry; you are right; but I have a reason, the kingdom of God is near.'

Though somewhat childish these dialogues sometimes have all the depth of the gospel. On 10 September 1987 R received this invitation:

'God loves you all.... Love him in return a little more; but God does not want a proud love.' In spite of some explanation R does not understand:

'He does not ask you to perform miracles; he requires that simple love which no one else can give in your place!'

On 13 September R returned to the question:

'I did not understand what you meant by proud love *(amore superbo)*'. She received the following response:

> This is what proud love means. I am going to tell you a story. A man sits on the front bench of the church and says, 'Lord, I did a good turn for such a family, I did such and such good deed.' Then he lists for the Lord all the good deeds he has done and at the end he concludes: 'Lord, I have loved you very much, more than others have loved you because I have done much good. Now you must love me more than you love others'.
>
> Another man comes in. He sits in the back of the church, lifts his hands to heaven and says, 'Lord, I am a sinner but I love you. Forgive me.' And a little later on he says, 'Lord, I have offended you by my sins and I know that I have not loved you enough, but please pardon me.' The Lord my God preferred the sinner to the other man who tempted God by listing his own virtues.

On hearing this story I asked R if she had not heard of the parable of the Pharisee and the Publican. She did not understand my question. I asked her parents to repeat it to her. But still she did not understand that what she had received was an updated version of this parable adapted to her comprehension.

One day in August the Virgin invited her to read the message which she had written:

'How is it that you have not left as you normally do?' R asked her.

'I will remain here until the message is read' (29 August 1987).

The parish priest was embarrassed because the bishop had asked him not to read the messages. He prayed for a solution but he did not read the message. He asked R to inquire from the Virgin how he should solve this dilemma. How could he obey her without disobeying the bishop?

On the following day he got this answer:

'Don A did well to obey his bishop. It was a trial and he overcame it well.'

On 1 October she received the following message which, in spite of the awkwardness of the style, gives food for thought:

> My children, how I love you! I love your sick heart. I love the dark colour of your soul. I love you because you are my children. You were all born in my womb. All humanity was in my womb but it grew so much that it could no longer remain within it. Then God created the Church: a people in which his children could live, a house that was like a mother. I lived in paradise and my children lived in peace on earth. One day my son called me urgently and said to me: 'My mother, return to earth, your children are on the point of being contaminated by a general malady within the house which I created for them (the Church).' I returned to earth but it was too late. The virus was everywhere and very few of you succeeded in returning to my womb. Very few have been cured or are on the way to being cured. The malady still exists and it is great. It has gone beyond its permitted bounds. If we do not succeed in stopping the virus, it will lead to the destruction of all life and God will abandon his children. Go with my blessing.

The style is symbolic, that of a parable; the message is adapted to the intelligence of a little girl and to her writing skills, but it is always the same message of love, prayer and conversion in a world situation that is becoming more serious. There is a strange and curious convergence with Medjugorje and Fatima.

On 3 October 1987 R received a message for the children. The rumpus they created was disturbing the adult prayer group. They were asked to pray in a different place. She took them apart and the results were excellent, both for themselves and for the adult group.

> 'Before beginning to pray I desire that you consecrate yourselves to my Immaculate Heart and to the sacred Heart of Jesus.'
>
> 'All that as well', replied R, who felt overwhelmed.
>
> 'That seems too much to you, little child,' she smiled.

'Well, I am going to reveal a secret to you'.

'What secret?'

'I promise that with your help I will save the world.'

'And Russia too?'

R knew of Russia because of a map which hung on the wall in her home.

'Russia will not be able to resist my power and I will make it resplendent with the light from my Immaculate Heart.'

It would be imprudent to give these apparitions any status. It would even be pretentious. R received a spiritual uplift, which was both joyous and painful, at a very critical moment in her development. It is still uncertain whether or not she is well-balanced. Her handwriting betrays strong emotional traits in her character which in fact may well be an element in the (final) explanation. Her handwriting shows a common desire to exist and be noticed. But she remains modest and discreet.

She comes from a family of four children. She is being reared by a Christian family in a parish where prayer is central. The parish priest is a brave and open man. He radiates holiness and good sense. R's still embryonic charism is bearing fruit, especially in the case of the children. Her development is being nurtured in the best conditions for her. No doubt her charism has a local function for the life of prayer of the parish and especially for the little children she is initiating into a life of prayer and encounter with God. May she remain in this modest situation and continue to play this humble role which is proving so beneficial to her family and to her parish, which, in its turn, continues to support her.

What has been of interest to me in this case has been the ambiguity on the one hand and on the other the excellent pastoral guidance which offers the best chances of success.

Notes

1. Robert Faricy and Luciano Pecoraio, *Maria in mezzo di noi, Le apparizioni di Oliveto Citra,* Padua, Messagero, 1987, 128p.

2. *La Regina dell'Amore:* S. Martino di Schio, A Cura del gruppo San Martino, Rome, Edic, 1987, 146pp: The origin and message of the apparitions at Schio.

3

WEEPING STATUES

Akita (Japan), 1973-81

In Akita[1] the event is not an apparition but a weeping statue.

Agnes Sasagawa Katsuko was born in 1931 and had been ill since her childhood. She had spent several spells in hospital. At the age of twenty-five she was cured of one of her childhood illnesses on drinking Lourdes water but seventeen years later (16 May 1973) she lost her hearing. She was a catechist who joined the convent of the Servants of the Eucharist at Akita, 200 kilometres north of Tokyo on the west coast. While she was praying before a statue of the Virgin on 12 June 1973 she became aware of a strange light. On 5 July the statue bled. From 29 September it was covered in perspiration and gave off a scent of lilies and roses and, finally, wept. There were 101 incidents from 4 January 1975 until 15 September 1981. The number was alleged to have the following meaning:

> Just as through a woman, sin entered the world, so also through a woman salvation has come into the world. The zero means: God is eternal. The first digit represents Eve, the second, the Virgin Mary. *(Apparition of 8 September 1981)*

The tears and the blood were closely related to the suffering of Sr Agnes and to the sin of the world.

'Pray in reparation for the sins of humanity, you will soon get better', she heard on 6 July 1973.

On 27 July Sr Agnes' hand bled painfully during a Mass celebrated by the Bishop. She heard the following words:

> Your sufferings are coming to an end today. Hold on to the precious memory of the blood of Mary. It is a call for conversion, peace and reparation for the outrages which men commit against God.

On 3 August at 3.00 p.m. she heard:
> I request your community to live in poverty, to sanctify itself and to pray in reparation for the ingratitude and outrages

of so many men. Are you really ready to sacrifice yourself in return? Take your vows in the knowledge that you will be nailed to the cross if you wish to be a worthy spouse of the Bridegroom.

29 September (the first perspiration):
Mary is even more sad than when she wept and bled. Wipe her perspiration.

13 October 1973:
The loss of so many souls makes me sad. If sin continues to become more serious and to multiply, there will not be further pardon.

Sr Agnes was cured of her deafness in two stages—on 13 October 1974 and on 30 May 1982.

The local bishop is favourably disposed to the events. He had to face the opposition of a nationally appointed commission of the other Japanese bishops and of the reticence of Rome which he visited twice. Before retiring (due to his age) he was allowed to proclaim the authenticity of the events.

I feel that Akita should be included in this brief overview not only because it is one of the few recent phenomena to have received official approval but also because it fits the pattern of the effusions at Damascus and because there are messages from Our Lady. The message in fact forms part of the context of Cardinal Sin's question: 'What does Our Lady wish to say to us?' — though here we have words without an apparition. The message however is the same conversion, the need for sacrifice and reparation:

Do not fear! Pray in reparation for the sins of all mankind. The modern world wounds the most sacred heart of Our Lord and Mary's wound is far deeper than your own *(Message from her guardian angel to Sr Agnes).*

On 3 August 1973 at 3.00 p.m. the voice announced chastisements that would befall humanity in surprisingly plain and popular language. The terms were analogous to those used at La Salette.

In order to show his anger, the heavenly Father is preparing to inflict a heavy chastisement on all humanity; I have intervened several times to appease the wrath of the Father; I have been able to withhold calamities by offering him the sufferings of his Son on the cross, his precious blood and those beloved souls who console him, who form the cohort of the victim souls. Prayer, penance and courageous sacrifice may soften the Father's anger; I ask this also of your community.

On 22 April 1984, Mgr John Shojiro ITO, Bishop of Niigata declared:

These facts, which have been established after eleven years of study, are undeniable .... Consequently I authorise the veneration of Our Lady of Akita.

Naju (Korea): Ongoing since 30 June 1985

Among the current phenomena there is also a case of a weeping statue in Naju in Korea. The phenomenon began on 30 June 1985 at 11.50 p.m. Naju is about 350 kilometres south-west of Seoul and to the south of Kwanju (population 1 million). Julio Kim is forty and he is married to Julia Youn who is thirty-nine. (In Korea women always retain their own names after marriage.) They have four children and are recent converts to Catholicism. They had a 50cm high statue of the Virgin on top of a wardrobe.

Julia had been sick and depressed. 'Why should I suffer so much?' she asked herself. A priest gave her the following advice: 'Bear with your sufferings, they are a bigger grace than getting better.' Then Jesus showed her his passion and asked her to join her sufferings with his.

On 29 June 1985 she visited the elderly sick; she returned home very tired but nevertheless recited the rosary. It was then that she saw the tears flowing from the eyes of the statue for the first time. News of the event spread quickly. Some days there were more than 3,000 visitors — and this in a country where only four per cent of the population is Catholic. The police became anxious. The tears were abundant for two or three months, then they became less frequent. Julio and Julia found a different apartment on the second floor of a four-storey block in a cooperative housing scheme. On the advice of the Virgin Julia gave up her position as manager of the local hairdressing salon which had many of the local prostitutes among its clientele. The messages Julia was given called for prayer, conversion, penance and reparation and there were special messages for priests.

At first the tears were ordinary. Then on 19, 20 and 21 October 1986 the tears were of blood. It was Julia's nine-year-old daughter, Therese, who first noticed this. On 25 October there was a mixture of ordinary tears and tears of blood.

Photographs of the event were shown at a priests' meeting by the local parish priest, Fr Johan Park Hi-dong; the matter was discussed. He was told:

'Take the statue home with you and then we'll see if the tears continue to flow.'

On 5 November 1986 he brought the statue to the presbytery. It was an enormous sacrifice for Julio and Julia. The statue stopped weeping. Then on 2 February a Belgian missionary, Fr Raymond Spies, had the following advice for the parish priest:

'The statue belongs to Julio and Julia. It is to Julia that the Virgin makes her wishes known. The fact that she does not weep in the presbytery just means that that is not her place!'

The parish priest brought back the statue and on its return to Julia's apartment the tears began again — water and blood. This was during the period from February to March. On 23 April the statue wept for almost seven hours, from midday to 7.00 p.m.; first there were ordinary tears and then after a pause the tears were of blood.

'Pray for priests all over the world', she said to Julia. The object of her prayer and her compassion is the lonely life of priests, the criticisms to which they are subjected and the sense of abandonment they are made to feel.

On 10 May the Virgin wept during the night, from 10.00 p.m. until 8.00 a.m. in the presence of two people, Julia and a woman who was visiting her. Towards midnight, before going to bed, they recited the act of consecration. A short time later Julia was assailed by the most horrendous pains; she felt they enabled her to share in Our Lady's sufferings. 'The pains babies feel in their mothers' wombs at the moment of abortion', was her description as she lay flat on the floor. The next day she had difficulty walking. There were other phenomena during the following days.

Crowds of visitors came to the apartment for the second anniversary of the tears on 30 June 1987. The parish priest celebrated Mass at 11.00 p.m. before the statue which had been weeping for some hours. The weeping continued during the Mass. There were over 300 people present in the apartment and on the stairs. The neighbours were being disturbed. From that time Julio and Julia began to look for premises large enough to accommodate the many visitors. They have now acquired a place. On 24 July 1987 the statue wept again. To the question, 'Why?', Julia gives the following reply:

'The Virgin complained that, having shown signs of repentance, people are not persevering in reparation and mortification and their prayer life is mediocre. She requested that the Pope, bishops and priests be obeyed. She is suffering because of the errors that so pervade the Church.

The principal messages deal with prayer and conversion:

Recite the rosary with fervour for peace in the world and for the conversion of sinners.

The anarchic use of birth control is destroying the sacred character of human life. Abortions have to be stopped by all means available. We must pray for those parents who kill their children by abortion and for those who carry out abortions. Pray and make reparation.

Pray incessantly for priests, my favourite sons. Satan is using all his wiles against them. They are assailed by temptations. The windows of the presbyteries are open to three temptations: pride, cupidity and luxury. Close the windows of the presbyteries. Sacrifices and perseverance in prayer are necessary to destroy Satan's efforts. Let all families resist evil. Revive the holiness of the family. Love each other. Be one just as the Father, Son and Holy Spirit are one. Be humble and be of one mind.

There are too many sacrilegious communions. Make reparation for the sufferings heaped upon my Son. Make known the importance of confession and communion.

Do not judge others (Mt 7:1). Many are being lost by falsely judging others (no date).

The weeping has recently become irregular. Over the past months the following have taken place: 18 August, ordinary tears;

15 September (the Feast of the Seven Dolours), tears of blood; 19 October, ordinary tears. On that day Julia was asked to share in the sorrows of Jesus Christ. She accepted and lost consciousness. Her body assumed the position of Jesus on the cross and blood appeared on the centre of her foot. This lasted for about one and a quarter hours.

After my visit of 8 December the tears continued until 26 December at 3.00 a.m. They reappeared on 13 January and lasted until 4 February. After this they disappeared until the spring. In the meantime Julia has twice experienced the stigmata in her hands: on 29 January and on 4 February.

The Archbishop of Kwanju is keeping a benevolent and watchful eye on everything. He has been as far as the entrance to the piece of ground where the chapel is located. They prefer to call it the hall of the Virgin rather than chapel, in order not to over-estimate anything. On the day of his visit the tears flowed again. A priest offered Julia a trip to Jerusalem at Easter; Jerusalem, the place of Christ's passion to which she now seems so profoundly and intimately linked.

What, then, should we think of this increase in astonishing phenomena all over the world? For some they are a source of annoyance, for others a cause of conversion. No doubt they are not central to belief; the essentials will always be the gospel, the Eucharist and the sacraments. Special signs from heaven must remain peripheral. But they do act as a stimulus and, sometimes against the odds, they bear fruit. To what extent is the increase in the numbers of these events due to improvement in communications or to a more benign attitude towards them? To what extent have the troubles of our times given rise to psychological factors which may have influenced this increase? To what extent has the gravity of the situation motivated the increase in these events with their urgent messages? There is no precise answer to these questions.

Apparitions in Lebanon
Mgr Elias Zoghby, a Greek Catholic bishop in the Lebanon, has himself translated from the Arabic and published the writings of Jeanne d'Arc Farage — *I have been seeing the Virgin for four years. Message to the world, to Lebanon and to the Church* — published by Éditions de l'Œil (4 rue Cassette, Paris 6e).

'Since Wednesday, 28 March 1984 (she writes) the Virgin has appeared to me regularly ... and has given me messages' (op. cit. p. 14).

Jeanne was eighteen when the apparitions began. She describes them herself. She had also seen Christ who associated her with his passion:

> The principal theme of the messages [she writes] is as follows: The sins of the world will quickly bring about a catastrophe. We must pray and do penance in union with Jesus Christ and his holy mother in order to help them save the world (p. 56).

A Lebanese priest has told me about other apparitions but I am not at liberty to speak about them. As far as he was concerned they posed serious problems because, after what appeared to be hopeful beginnings, they showed signs of what appeared to him to be satanic deviations. However, these subsequent weaknesses need not call into question the initial positive signs. Temptations and deviations are the major and constant risk of all apparitions. Lourdes itself had a brief epidemic of visionaries (11 April to 11 July 1858).

... and elsewhere

Recent travels have thrown up other alleged apparitions. One reason for this is that there is now greater freedom to speak about these matters which, for so long, were shrouded in enforced silence. The removal of articles forbidding free publication from the old Code of Canon Law may well be a factor in this. Christians should not abuse this new freedom through a lack of prudence, obedience or a proper critical sense. This is what causes a backlash. At the moment self-discipline and self-censorship are remarkable in the main places of apparition. This book would like to be of help in placing these spiritual phenomena in their real, but modest context.

Note:

1. Teiji Yasuda, *Notre-Dame d'Akita (Japon): Les Larmes et le message de Marie*, Hautville (CH 1631, Switzerland), Editions du Parvis, 1987, 236p.

Shimura Tatsuya, *La Vierge Marie au Japon: Akita*, ibid, 1985 48p.

Jim Jacq, *Celle qui pleure au Japon*, Téqui, 1983 and *J'ai vu pleurer ma mère à Akita* (Japon); these are incomplete but the author is preparing a new edition in English.

Convergence of the messages

Invitations to conversion
to a world in danger

1

MULTIPLICITY, VARIETY, DEMOCRATISATION OF APPARITIONS

What conclusion can be drawn from this overview? In the first instance, that there is an enormous variety of apparitions.

Diversity

Varying from case to case, the visionaries are children, adolescents and adults, men and women, single and married: Bernardo at Cuapa; Renato Baron at Schio; Maria Esperanza Medrano de Bianchini at Finca Betania; Gladys at San Nicolas; Amparo at Escorial; Myrna at Damascus. At Medjugorje three of the visionaries chose celibacy for the sake of the Kingdom; nevertheless Ivanka, who was engaged to be married prior to the apparitions went ahead with the marriage after five years of careful reflection and it would appear that Mirjana will do the same thing.

These facts give the lie to the received wisdom according to which visionaries are always children, young girls or shepherdesses. There is not even one shepherdess among the visionaries listed in this book. The statistics produced by Fr Besutti in respect of Italian visionaries from the thirteenth century onwards had already disproved this belief. The majority of them are in fact male adults; but proverbs seem to ignore the facts.

Another factor that leads to diversity is the apparitions' adaptation to each language, culture and country, etc. We have no stereotypical description regarding clothing or age. As in previous apparitions these differences are a sign of the freedom and powers of adaptation of glorified bodies. The signs are extremely varied; they include lights, scents, spiritual and physical cures, particularly at Finca Betania (Venezuela).

The missions are also varied: contemplative, evangelical and ecumenical. From many points of view the fruits are diverse. Again there is no stereotype, but, as always in a living Church, initiatives seem to burgeon and the fruits are structured from within: prayer, mutual help and commitment, adapted to the needs of the time.

Sometimes the apparitions give rise to a parochial cult and sometimes they are merely private, but this depends on the extent to which they are welcomed. The very fact of objection to an apparition marginalises the cult. But where priests prudently take this grace on board, with all its uncertainties, there is a better chance of a healthy evolution through the parish environment and the grace of the sacraments. This was one of the admirable features of Medjugorje: though the parish priest was initially sceptical he did all in his power to bring the people from the hill of the apparitions to the church for daily Mass. Little by little the apparitions became part of the daily Mass. The Virgin had led people to the Eucharist, but the skill of the parish priest had contributed enormously.

There are many different reactions. There are two series of alleged apparitions at Split. Both parish priests in question tended to marginalise the events. The first series of apparitions alleged to have taken place at Gala were so successfully marginalised that they are no longer even spoken of. There were other apparitions in another parish. The subject was a young man who was so far removed from the Church that he could scarcely recall the Our Father. During the apparitions a crowd gathered round him spontaneously. They were not able to fit in his house and this naturally drew the attention of the police; in that country religion is permitted only in church. These good Christians requested the parish priest to invite them one way or another into the church. He refused. However, the bishop, who had shown an interest in the events, wrote to the parish priest and asked him to receive the people into the church without any commitment, by way of emergency solution as it were. He then put a gifted priest in charge of the visionary and the group, who, through their association with him, had rediscovered their faith. At least that bishop understood that it was more important to provide proper pastoral guidance than to set up a commission of inquiry.

A turning point
The frequency and diversity of the apparitions described would seem to mark a turning point. Lately, whenever there is an apparition that on the face of it looks genuine, the question is immediately raised: will it be a new Lourdes, a new Fatima? Of course the model was established in a certain number of cases where officially approved apparitions tended to become major events in the Church. The biggest sanctuaries in the world (after

Rome) are in Guadalupe (Mexico), Lourdes and Fatima. A new apparition seemed to herald a new high-point for the Church. This is an illusion caused by a lack of perspective. There are plenty of small sanctuaries associated with apparitions which have remained regional or local: Laus, Garaison, Pellevoisin, Saint-Bauzille de la Sylve, etc. Thus those apparitions that emerged from the crucible appeared to be of such stature that people automatically thought that every apparition would be of universal importance. But the very frequency of apparitions and the modest stature of some among them shows clearly that we are dealing with rather modest phenomena, many of them private, and that Guadalupe, rue du Bac, Lourdes or Fatima are the exceptions.

So the present multiplicity of apparitions leads us to a proper understanding of their status: small signs from heaven given for the time being in one place or another and by no means always requiring the erection of a sanctuary. Where there are sanctuaries they are frequently small and of local importance. Apparitions have suffered because too much was made of them. The proliferation which has made them popular is in itself healthy. Perhaps we should speak of a democratisation of apparitions?

Is there an overall strategy?

There is a strongly held view that present-day apparitions are a phase in Our Lady's organic plan which is unfolding from Guadalupe through the Miraculous Medal right up to our own times. According to this view each apparition is like a single piece of a jigsaw puzzle or the single notes of a symphony which need to be put together. This view has always appeared to me to be artificial and even dangerous.

To me apparitions seem like individual cries from heaven, heard in various places at various times without any overall plan. Our Lady's familiarity intervenes to particularise and personalise the Christian message according to our needs.

2

HARMONY AND CONVERGENCE

Reading the gospel message

All apparitions presumed to be authentic adapt the gospel message for today. In saying this one can almost anticipate the objections: you are diminishing the apparitions, you are making of them a simple repetition of the gospel, eliminating in principle all that is particular to them. You are softening the focus, making the cutting edge blunt and reducing them to a state of relativity. You are reducing them to nothing.

The focus has to be properly set. We are not dealing with objective novelty but with prophetic innovation. The cutting edge is that of a particular time and a particular place. These localised, personalised challenges adapt the message of the gospel — which in substance is complete and definitive — to new situations. The word 'adapt' is not really strong enough because the prophetic message of the apparitions does more: it makes known the hidden potential of the gospel which will continue to be revealed in the future, no matter how long the world goes on. Prophecy (speaking in the name of God) stands out in clear relief in the testimonies of the visionaries. Prophecy has existed throughout the history of the Church and is her future.

These are important observations. If we were to forget that the revelation of Christ, his sacraments and his gospel are the essentials we would quickly lapse into a lop-sided religion of apparitions, a religion which would be impaired, impoverished and disintegrated.

The wisdom and the relevance of certain messages goes beyond the ken of the visionaries. We have already noted the contrast between the modest, hesitant speech of Myrna when she gives her personal account of things, and the rapid assurance with which she dictates the messages which she has received. She dictates them rapidly, for her memory, like that of Bernadette before her, is not always to be trusted.

The dual function of the message

Then there is the dual function of the messages and the two kinds of messages.

1. The permanent function is to reawaken faith and to bring about a return to God, to prayer and to fasting. It is a return to the introductory chapters of the gospel, to the preaching of John the Baptist for conversion and the baptism of repentance.

These messages are repetitive. There are those who have criticised their banality; but this is normal — they have an educational function and education always requires repetition.

Some messages are impressive because of their clarity, relevance, topicality and depth or their harmonious and persuasive conformity with the gospel. The most striking and astonishing messages are not always the most important ones. Sometimes the most banal messages can move mountains in a person's life and bear extraordinary fruits in the long term. The modest invitation to fast on bread and water twice a week, which issued from Medjugorje, has reached hundreds of thousands of Christians all over the world and, little by little, has changed their hygiene, health, lifestyle and their prayer life.

The thing which all the messages associated with apparitions have in common is that they bear witness to the living and transcendent presence of the Lord and invite us to take him seriously. They are an invitation to dialogue. Indeed many apparitions are limited to this essential aspect.

2. Other messages are marked in varying degrees by their prophetic impact. In 1531 Our Lady of Guadalupe reminded the conquering Spaniards that in the eyes of God an Indian is equal to a Spaniard and can take messages from heaven to a bishop. This topples the one-sided hierarchy that may exist between the person who commands and the one who obeys because in the first instance we must all obey God. Our Lady made it clear that the Church in Latin America was, first and foremost, to be a home for the natives, and only then for the colonisers. The gospel gives priority to the poor. This was a pertinent reminder in the context of the savage, unChristian violence of a war of conquest.

Rue du Bac reminded a desolate world of the closeness of heaven; it was a world which the Revolution had deChristianised, secularised and orphaned. At the same time Our Lady gave back confidence to a Church that was still nursing the wounds inflicted by the Revolution. She awakened the prayer, initiative and missionary zeal of a century that was to become exemplary.

La Salette had a more special effect on the material life of the peasant population. Our Lady used the potato blight as her starting point; for them this was an absolutely eloquent sign, whatever the wise might have made of it.

Lourdes came to remind the world of the value of evangelical poverty. It was a world where money was a god and the rule was 'Get rich'. Power and the ability to get elected were dependent on wealth and were thus restricted to the privileged few. These apparitions brought forth a tiny saint of enormous stature from the poorest and most lowly stratum of society.

During the First World War Fatima was a salutary reminder that peace comes only from God, from his love manifested in the Immaculate Heart of Mary. What was urgent was the conversion of atheists, including those adherents of Marxist atheism which was being systematically instilled in the USSR. A world which, through sin, was bent on war was offered a new direction through a return to the Lord.

There were two aspects to the message — a prophetic statement about the future with its dangers and most immediate urgencies, and a reminder of the gospel message. The answer to the problems and risks of the world is always the same; it is not that of the sphinx so beloved of André Gide, who believed that the answer to every great question is always the same — man and man alone.

The Bible and the gospel also state that the solution lies in one word. But it is not the same word; the revealing word is God who is our creator and without whom we will not be saved.

Present-day apparitions plough the same furrow as the gospels and the apparitions of earlier centuries. So, finally, we are in a position to understand the ambitious question posed by Cardinal Sin and to offer a response.

3

WHAT IS OUR LADY SAYING IN HER CURRENT APPARITIONS?

Like previous apparitions those of today are at one and the same time a prophetic message and an evangelical response. The response may appear to be repetitive, even banal. We have heard it before. However, the prophetic warning shakes us out of our inertia. It makes us look more seriously at a reality we have neglected and forgotten, because for us the urgent often displaces the essential.

The message of the apparitions offers us in the first place a diagnosis: our modern world has abandoned itself happily and quietly to sin. It is destroying itself. The threats are serious. This is what the apparitions are saying in different ways, sometimes in a language intended to shock, at other times in a secret elliptical language as in the case of Medjugorje where all that is known are the threats and their causes (sin and forgetfulness of God) and the remedies. Other apparitions alluded to the murderous divisions which are tearing Central America apart or, indeed, to the threat of a third world war (Cuapa, Escorial etc.)

This diagnosis has to be seen in a historical context. The world believed that it had found the secret of happiness by abandoning God. At the beginning of the twentieth century triumphant scientists proclaimed that the infallible progress of science and reason would create the peace, prosperity and health which humanity had previously requested from God. Science was going to put an end to disease, famine and war. This misleading conviction was shortlived. The century, believed to be the threshold of a golden age, went on to create two world wars and the threat of a third which even now is being prepared for. Our world has become the theatre for an unprecedented explosion of violence. Moral deviation has been responsible for the appearance of new diseases for which there is still no known cure. Never have so many suffered from malnutrition while at the same time illnesses attributable to over-indulgence in food and abuse of drugs have never been more rampant.

The apparitions soften and to some degree filter the proclamation of imminent threats ('death is coming' — San

Nicolas; 'The world is at the edge of a precipice'—Kibeho), because the intention is not to frighten people or increase their anxieties, but rather to invite them back to the source which will heal their ills and anxieties.

International experts and world leaders are only too aware of the diagnosis but they are better at reassuring public opinion than at solving the problem. Over the decades the best they have done to promote peace is to create 'a balance of fear' which in turn has led to the arms race. Deadly arsenals of biological, chemical and atomic weapons have been stockpiled, enough arms to destroy the entire planet. The softened and filtered messages of the apparitions do not elaborate on this dreadful prospect — it is self-evident in any case — but point to the root·cause of the evil and to its remedy.

The root of evil is sin (insult to God and the destruction of humanity). The many facets of our lack of love undermine the family (Medjugorje). In our western countries the number of marriages is on the decrease while there has been a marked increase in the number of divorces. In a society founded on the principle of pleasure, where one seeks pleasure without conception and where conception is achieved without giving birth, we have all too frequently forgotten the meaning of fidelity and self-giving, the cornerstones both of the family and of society.

To a world bent on war, violence and divisions the messages issue an urgent call to peace and reconciliation: 'I am the reconciliation of the peoples' (Finca Betania). 'I have come to ask for peace' (Terra Blanca). 'Peace' (Medjugorje). It is precisely here that we rejoin the eternal message of the gospel: God, the source and final end of all peace; faith in and conversion to him alone; prayer.

And for our affluent western countries, to the invitation to prayer is added a more unusual message, the invitation to fasting which lays the foundations for prayer, evangelical poverty and peace.

Thus, present-day apparitions do nothing more than underline the parlous state of our world and the urgent necessity of returning to God and to the key concepts of the gospel.

Chastisement?

A message that is meant to shock, one might say. A message of practical self-interest. Punishments are threatened, because sin is not the way to success; it makes us do evil. By returning to God we have the means of putting an end to our troubles.

To understand the messages in this way is to be very wide of the mark. It is true that the word 'chastisement' or 'punishment' is used in the messages of Oliveto Citra and Medjugorje. But this is just a manifestation of the elementary nature of their language which, nevertheless, is in the best of biblical traditions. In the *Jerusalem Bible* the word 'punishment', is used sixty-two times and the verb 'to chastise' is used ninety times.

However, the interpretation referred to at the outset is a caricature of the biblical concept. The Bible teaches us to prefer God to his gifts, to look on him with love and not as a magician. The messages retain what is essential: sin is evil in the first place because it wounds God's love. More concretely, sin was the cause of Christ's Passion, the mysterious and transcendent everlasting nature of which is recalled in the messages. The permanent scandal remains: the Son of God (God himself) has been wounded, put to death in his humanity by the sin of the world, our sin. This death is not something that happened in the past. It is forever present through the eternity of the Son of God. The human sufferings of his passion are forever contemporary because of his eternal 'I'. This is what is made concrete by the Virgin's tears, sometimes tears of blood because sin, more than it may appear, is a bleeding and bloody evil. 'My son suffers from the multitude of sins' (Terra Blanca, see pp. 61-62). We now understand why she uses the present tense.

As regards the word 'chastisement', it is a word that needs interpreting in the messages as in the Bible. The language is anthropomorphic, based on the image of rearing a child or even training an animal. Today these words are looked on with horror, often excessively so. Some bishops have said of AIDS that it is not a punishment, but a medical and technical problem. What is true in this rather one-sided conclusion is that God does not punish from the outside, as it were, out of a sense of vengeance. He created a good world and submitted it to humanity: 'And God said to them, ''Be fruitful and multiply, and fill the earth and subdue it; and have dominion over the fish of the sea and over the birds of the air ...'' ' *(Gen 1:28)*. To this end 'he left him in the power of his own inclination' *(Sir 15:14)*; he gave him freedom so that he could rule over the kingdom.

Our sin destroys the order and the ecology of divine creation. We develop and degrade the world over which we rule. Ecologists are aware of this at the level of the natural rhythms of the world. But there is not sufficient awareness at the level of moral and religious balance through which creation has an essential relationship with the creator, and humankind, under pain of self-destruction, a similar relationship with God. In endeavouring to cut ourselves off from the creator, we are like a woodcutter who saws off the branch on which he is sitting. This moral and divine balance is, in the final analysis, the most important aspect. For this reason we should try to go beyond Freudian psychoanalysis with its emphasis on the control of basic drives. We should re-invent a more essential psychoanalysis, which in its time was well-known to spiritual directors, and which would re-establish equilibrium from above, and thus the fundamental relationship of the creature with the creator, which should be rendered objectively and fruitfully conscious. By destroying the relationship of the creature with the creator sin destroys the creature itself. Through sin we are wounded, psychically, bodily and spiritually and the world is destroyed. The evidence is as clear as day. Abuse of alcohol tends to destroy the alcoholic organically and only those with the strongest lungs escape the ravages of smoking. Sexual promiscuity and perversion have led to dreadful diseases. And this is not the full story. At a deeper level our lust for money, for power and for pleasure has debased both the sinner and society. The idealist cult of human subjectivity, the 'pleasure principle', gives rise to disorder and to violence.

None of this is vengeance poured out from above but is the intrinsic consequence of human error. Self-destruction is a form of immanent justice. It is not God who is the author of evil, it is we ourselves.

We should not forget that, because of human solidarity, evil extends even to the innocent. We cannot therefore identify punishment with crime. We must show understanding and mercy to all who suffer no matter what the origin of the suffering. Christ did not choose one person more than another but he did give priority to sinners; he had a strange preference for the one lost sheep over the ninety-nine others. Mother Teresa, whose priority is for the poor, has opened a clinic for AIDS sufferers. She makes no distinction between the sinner and the innocent, between those who are the authors of their own suffering and those who are the victims of a raging contagion. Each person gets the same loving care, without discrimination, though there is no encouragement of the sins that are at the root of the evil.

Once more, it would not be doing justice to the messages if we were to reduce them to the theory of immanent justice, of crime and punishment. The overriding message is that sin crucifies Christ; this is the supreme and permanent scandal from which all others flow.

Alarmist?

Another apparent scandal lies in the fact that the messages do not offer an escape from the most dramatic consequences of sin. At Medjugorje we are told that these consequences can be reduced and modified but not entirely avoided. Our Lady said that prayer and penance had in fact reduced the threats contained in the eighth secret. We have already noted that, even in the case of the saints, predictions are not infallible; they are not given to satisfy our curiosity but to advance human history, the history of salvation. What is clearly promised is a deep sense of peace to those who live with the Lord. Even through the sorrows of this world, nothing can take away peace from those who live with God.

The end of the world?

The messages concerning the future of the world would appear to predict the end of the world (Mirjana at Medjugorje). However, remember the words of Jesus: 'But of that day or that hour no one knows, not even the angels in heaven, nor the Son, but only the Father' *(Mk 13:32)*. We must approach the interpretation of these prophetic utterances with great circumspection and prudence. The prophets tend to see the future according to a foreshortened perspective. Thus the early Christians expected to see the second coming of Christ at the hour of their own death (1 Th 4:13-18). Renato Baron had the same problems with perspective. Nevertheless when I asked him: 'Are you foretelling the end of the world?', he replied, 'No, the end of *a* world'. In the same way when Mirjana appears to envisage a second coming in the near future (the only one among the visionaries to do so), we have to be aware of this problem of perspective. It is certain that all the dramas and the evils of this world, and the death of each one of us are signs foretelling the end of the world. But are they proximate signs or signs of a more distant future? Nobody can answer this with certainty.

The challenge of the signs

Before concluding, there is another aspect of the apparitions which shocks the wise and the knowledgeable, including many theologians. The apparitions are adorned with concrete, elementary and simple signs: tears, blood, perspiration, oil, perfume and lights. These expressively tangible signs appeal to our ambivalent rational nature. Their language has a power beyond words.

Such a language might well appear weak and feeble to some intellectuals (particularly those who lack a sense of poetry). But it is at one with biblical language and leads us to the Bible. It is equally at one with the languages of love which endeavour to announce the ineffable. The over-intellectual mentality of our modern world finds it hard to come to grips with this. At the same time these signs are in line with the sacraments to which they give new vigour. This is in contrast with the abstract nature of certain ecclesiastical language, be it theological or administrative.

The outpouring of signs speaks to the heart. It recreates that attractiveness which administrative dullness had made us forget. We are reminded of one of the antiphons of Our Lady: *In odorem unguentorum currimus, Sancta Dei Genitrix* (We follow in the sweet odour of your perfumes, Holy mother of God).

On a deeper level, these messages and the apparitions themselves remind us that God is present, that he himself is close to us through his Mother, his angels and his saints who are his friends and his servants. Theology correctly insists on the transcendence of God. It often does this in extremely abstract language. Because of the insistence on the fact that God is 'Other' we tend to forget the equally important point that he has made us in his own image and likeness, through a sharing of his nature which is an invitation to friendship. No matter how transcendent he is, God does resemble us in some respects. This is the way he has made us. He is simultaneously transcendent and familiar and our forgetfulness of this divine familiarity is inimical to the attractiveness of the Christian life, the encounter and dialogue with God.

The visionaries have a feeling for this familiarity. Alphonse Ratisbonne, the visionary associated with the Miraculous Medal, gave a striking and spontaneous expression of this on the occasion of his visit to Pope Gregory XVI on 3 February 1842:

> I had never appeared before the leaders of this world and these great people appeared very small to me in comparison with the true grandeur [of the Pope]. I freely admit that all the majesties of the world seemed to be concentrated in him who here below possesses the power of God .... I will never forget how I was overwhelmed by fear as I entered the Vatican and went through so many courtyards and so many imposing halls on my way to the Pope's rooms. But all my anxiety gave way to astonished surprise when I saw the man himself, so simple, so humble and so fatherly. He was not a monarch but a father who, in his extreme goodness, treated me like a beloved child.
>
> My God! Will it be like this on the last day when I have to appear before you? ... We tremble at the thought of the grandeur of God and we are anxious about his justice; but because of his great mercy confidence will prevail and with that confidence love and thankfulness without end.
>
> (*Mémoire*, entry for 12 April 1842, 1919 edition, p. 94, the last entry.)

Thus God visited Adam at the break of day (Gen 3:8). All those who meet the visionaries are touched by the familiarity, the simple and almost naive manner in which they speak to the Virgin, and they emerge with a healthier view of our relationship with heaven. It is a family relationship where communications are easy. It is the relationship of the body which we form in Christ, that of one living being.

The messages are frequently marked by simplicity, poverty and evangelical freshness in contrast to the wisdom of those who so knead and flatten the gospel that they destroy it by reducing it to human sciences or ideologies which never lead to a personal encounter. The function of all these signs (cures, lights, solar phenomena, emissions of oil and perfumes) is to invite us to a personal encounter. Whether in the Bible or in apparitions, the God we meet in a twilight zone uses a language that is simple and non-rational (though always remarkably coherent). Those whose lives are ruled by love grasp the inner, irreplaceable meaning of this language.

But let us return to the essentials of the message.

4

OTHER ASPECTS OF THE MESSAGE

The prophetic impact of the messages associated with recent apparitions is new when compared to rue du Bac, La Salette, Lourdes, etc. They underline evangelisation and ecumenism and remind us of the priority to be given to the poor.

Evangelisation
The message of a return to God, repeated in a number of apparitions (most explicitly at Cuapa, Kibeho, Damascus and Schio), takes the form of an invitation to evangelisation which is characterised by a dynamic and joyful urgency. This evangelisation radiates to millions of pilgrims who visit the parish of Medjugorje. Segatasha radiates the same evangelisation into the neighbouring areas of Rwanda. Our Lady of Damascus invites us to proclaim 'my Son, Emmanuel' (God with us). This teaching confirms the urgency of the evangelisation of which the Church has become conscious through other means since the fourth Synod in 1974. It has been and is still being put into practice by Popes Paul VI and John Paul II.

Ecumenism
Certain apparitions approve and encourage ecumenism. One such instance is the apparitions in Egypt where Our Lady appeared to a fraternal gathering of Catholic and Coptic Christians and Muslims, who actually recognise Our Lady in the Koran. The convergence between Damascus and Medjugorje rests on the fact that they both deal with an ecumenism based on love, without which smiles, dialogue and negotiation would all be in vain. This particular angle of the message is somewhat disconcerting and at the same time far-reaching (René Laurentin, *Messages et Pedagogie de Marie à Medjugorje,* pp. 317-322).

Moreover it is in this same spirit that the apparitions invite evangelisation: an evangelisation without aggression, proselytism or recourse to the techniques of the media (because media techniques usually treat evangelisation in a superficial manner), but one using the power of God and the super-abundant gift of prayer. This type of evangelisation is self-disseminating where it is based not on the psychological sciences (which belong to the surface), but on God himself who goes to the heart of the matter and confounds the wisdom of the wise.

The priority of the poor

Current apparitions underline to various degrees a priority of the poor which was already indicated at Lourdes, rediscovered by the Council and is being further emphasised by Pope John Paul II.

In the first place this is indicated by the choice of visionaries. Ordinarily they are from a simple, usually agricultural background, close to the nature which inspires many of the gospel parables.

We use the word 'poor' in the gospel sense: stripping oneself of the goods and possessions of this world. We often find in the visionaries and in their families an *'aurea mediocritas'*. They are content with their meagre lot. The peasant workers in Medjugorje lead a hard life which alternates between the tobacco fields and the vineyards. This does not always provide a good living and Vicka's father had to emigrate to Germany to find work and support his family. This was a tragic solution to the problem but the family accepted it with resignation. Because of a disease in the plant, the tobacco crop is in trouble and is almost at an end. This is not the place to go into the economic consequences of this for the village. The arrival of the pilgrims and the building of house extensions to accommodate them has taken up the slack left by the demise of the tobacco trade.

Thus the visionaries live in poverty but not necessarily in misery. The visionary of Escorial experienced the most tragic circumstances. What is remarkable about her is that even in these tragic conditions she was able to maintain the spirit of the poor according to the gospel. The modest condition of the visionaries has done nothing to raise the prestige of the apparitions in the eyes of the important people of the Church or the state. They tend to look down on the naivety of the visionaries and on their rustic background and the lack of precision in their language which has none of the rigour of theology or the human sciences. They are not aware that these poor people often have a nobility which is due to the quality of their lives and their humanity.

But heaven gives us the same message that it had already given at Lourdes. In 1858 the miserable condition of the Soubirous family and the disdain in which they were held did nothing to facilitate the acceptance of the apparitions. Peyramale reacted badly to Bernadette's first visit. She was accompanied by two aunts who had been dismissed from the Children of Mary for having conceived before their marriages. The other visionaries, who came from better backgrounds and were in fact Children of Mary, were given a much better welcome. But it was quickly seen where God's choice lay. Antoinette Tardhivail, a young woman from Lourdes, was already writing on 29 March 1858: 'Bernadette is very poor; she is as poor as was Our Lord when he was on earth. But it is on this young girl that Our Lady has looked favourably in preference to so many other rich people who at this moment envy the lot of someone whom they would have despised but are now happy to embrace her or even touch her hand'. (René Laurentin, *Lourdes. Récit authentique,* Paris, 1966, pp. 255-256). Four years later the magisterium in the person of the bishop drew the same conclusion, quoting from St Paul: ' "But God chose what is foolish in the world to shame the wise, God chose what is weak in the world to shame the strong" *(1 Co 1:27):* a fourteen-year-old born of very poor parents' (Episcopal mandate of 18 January 1862).

The lesson which seemed so evident then is far from being understood in our time. We tend to look down on the visionaries, and the extraordinary sanctity which is evident, both in them and in their families, is looked on as weakness. As a means of overcoming the embarrassment they caused there was little hesitation in labelling them as hallucinating or hysterical. Any theologian who pretends to find some light in this kind of nonsense would himself be despicable. Those who follow the apparitions closely are impressed by the sanctity of the poor and by their fruits among the people of God.

5

THE DEEP MEANING OF THE MESSAGE

While alerting a world in danger the multiple messages from Our Lady remind us that God is the final solution to all our problems; the apparitions remind us of the simultaneous familiarity and transcendence of God and of his indispensable presence.

In the first instance they remind us of God the creator and of our often forgotten condition as creatures. Creation is not something that happened in the past, an act by which God projected the world into existence. Creation is the permanent act by which God gives existence to everything at every moment of its being. Thus he has a more intimate relationship with us than we have with ourselves.

But our condition is not one of dependence alone because God has created us autonomous and free. Our condition is not one of subjection, because God is our Father. He created us from love and destined us for love. The God whom we have forgotten is therefore the Good News.

While our condition reminds us of the transcendence of God, it is also a sign of his immanence and closeness. Between the creator and the creature is an indissoluble bond. We should not forget the very real familiarity which characterises our relationship with God: from Abraham through the prophets to Mary; from Francis of Assisi to Thérèse of Lisieux and the visionaries who have this experience which, far from being frightening or destructive, is simple and gratifying.

Mary too is a creature like ourselves made in the image of God. She is the most beautiful human image of God. It is an image of God in his mercy, a feminine image which is as like to God as a masculine image, for God is neither male nor female. In him these images harmonise concretely.

God commissioned Mary to his Son so that she might familiarise him with humankind. He then sent her to us so that she would familiarise us with God. She is a privileged manifestation of the mercy of God among us. For this purpose, she was given her vocation as mother of humanity at the foot of the cross. Let us listen to her as she reminds us ceaselessly of what we have forgotten to read in the gospel.

As St Catherine Labouré has said, the Virgin of the Incarnation leaning over the crib, the Virgin of Cana and the Virgin of the apparitions is one and the same. She continues to intercede for us before Christ saying: 'They have no wine'. They have exhausted the wellsprings of joy for which they were made. She continues to repeat to us what she said to the servants of Cana when she pointed to Christ: 'Do whatever he tells you' *(Jn 2:5)*.

Appendices

These appendices hold the residue of our enquiry.

1. Cases where information is insufficient:

a) Grouchevo in the USSR (see Appendix 1).
b) Turzovka, Czechoslovakia, where Matthias Laschut, a forty-two-year-old forest ranger, married with three children, had apparitions of Christ and Mary from 1 June to 14 August 1958. Communications are poor in the Eastern Bloc countries. Both witnesses and bishops live in fear. See S. Sensick, *Turzovka, Slevensky Lurd,* and its English translation; *Turzovka, Slovakian Lourdes,* Cambridge, Ontario, Jesuit House, PO Box 600, 80 pp. Also Francesco Grufik, *Turzovka, À Lourdes da Checoslovaquia,* Prague, Ed. Boa Nova, 1981.
c) Nigeria, 'the apparitions of Mary' to Felix Emeka Onah, known as *Servus Mariae* in the village of Ede-Oballa, Nsukka in the state of Anambra, since 17 January 1980. There is a need for further information. The visionary would appear to be in some difficulty with his bishop.
d) 'C', in the neighbourhood of Barcelona. Apparitions to an adult about which the bishop has requested silence.

2. Cases which show weaknesses or evident deviations and are therefore not credible. We will list them briefly without undermining those who may sincerely have deviated and later became aware of their mistakes. May they be helped on the road back to humble observance.

3. Cases of conflict which are on the way to extinction or are being carefully channelled.
  Two cases are worth noting:

4. Apparitions at Île Bouchard (1947)

5. The numerous messages received by Don Gobbi, founder of the Marian Priestly Movement.

Appendix 1

APPARITION OF THE VIRGIN AT GROUCHEVO IN THE USSR?

There is a huge amount of information which has to be approached with caution. This is something new in the USSR. Since Easter 1987 'apparitions of the Virgin' at Grouchevo (Hrouchiv, in Ukranian) have attracted many pilgrims. The police do not interfere. 'Is this yet another sign of the liberalisation going on under Mr Gorbachev?' asked *Le Monde* on 21 August 1987.

Membra disjecta

What then is happening at Grouchevo? Many things remain unclear, but a dossier drawn up by Serge Benoît, a specialist in Russian affairs, has thrown some light on the events.

It all began on the morning of 26 April 1987 on the anniversary of the Chernobyl disaster. At 8.00 a.m. Maria Kizyn, a fourth class student, and therefore about ten or eleven years old, came out of her house which is opposite a disued church.

'Suddenly', said her mother, 'she saw on one of the sides of the octagonal tower of the Church, a silhouette, a lady in black.' Perhaps the Virgin is in mourning for the USSR?

'The little one ran back into the house', the mother continued. 'Crowds came into the house and into the kitchen garden which stretches almost as far as the chapel. The potatoes had to be replanted three times. Each time they were trampled upon. A lot of foolishness has been doing the rounds about my daughter: It has even been claimed that she had been dumb from birth and that she had begun to speak after seeing the Virgin.'

From here on the mother's account peters out, apparently to prevent reprisals. It is difficult to get accurate information in a country where double-talk has become second nature. The chapel of the 'apparition' was constructed during a cholera epidemic on the site of a miraculous spring which had been venerated since the seventeenth century. Pilgrims used to come here three times a year to ask for pardon or beg for a cure. The church was closed down in 1959, during the Khrushchev era — a liberal period in many respects but not in relation to religion. Careful police control was enough to put an end to the pilgrimages.

The ambiguous language of an imprint

When the apparitions happened the chapel was locked with two strong padlocks. The keys were with the assistant to the president of the local soviet and he had transferred to another region. Visitors were able to look through a hole in the door through which they saw a gold painted wooden icon and the curbstone of the octagonal well. 'Moreover the authorities had erected a fence and dug a ditch around the chapel' (Quote from an anonymous pilgrim published in the *Bulletin*, Alexander Ogorodnikov's Christian publication). But another pilgrim quoted in the same organ contradicts this:

> We looked very carefully and we saw none of the things we had heard about in Moscow; there was no fence, no ditch and not a soldier in sight. There was no luminous statue of the Virgin with the child in her arms filtering through the planks. There were only a few pilgrims and trampled earth. If in fact there was a ditch on the other side it would have been used for draining the kitchen garden.

The first witness opens up an entirely different perspective:

> The authorities blocked up the windows and covered in the spring. The apparition appeared on the outside. On the Feast of the Ascension an image similar to an icon of the Virgin, holding the child in her arms, all bright and covered in stars, was seen above the church. After the Feast of the Ascension it climbed higher into the sky. At the beginning of June it was high up in the clouds but clearly visible (ibid.)

But the other pilgrim reduced this rather flowery evidence to more modest proportions:

> On one of the planks of the octagonal tower which supported the cupola one could distinguish a vague outline and the women present said that it was the imprint of the apparition. We had binoculars and we studied it. We could see old grey planks. They had become blackened with time and were stained by the rain. If you really wanted to and if you used a large dose of imagination, on one of the planks you could

distinguish the silhouette of a woman. But to be frank, if we had not known that there had been an apparition of the Virgin, we would not have put any interpretation on what we saw. If we had been asked what we were seeing we would have had difficulty in answering.

Two other pilgrims to Grouchevo, Ukrainians resident in Poland, confirm the objectivity of these remarks. The majority of the witnesses would appear to confirm that the apparitions ceased very quickly. There is only one vague witness as regards any message:

> The Virgin only spoke to children and disappeared as soon as adults arrived on the scene. She taught them the basics of their faith and also how to pray. On the last occasion she appeared in a mysterious aura of light with Christ in her arms and miraculously left her infant on one of the stained glass windows of the church. (This account was also published in the *Bulletin*.)

During a local television programme which featured a discussion on the apparitions, some viewers said that they saw the image of the Virgin on their screens on 13 May 1987, the seventieth anniversary of Fatima. But this is yet another twilight zone phenomenon which many people did not see. Other rumours had it that the Virgin showed herself on buildings in various towns and in particular on government buildings. But the very diversity of these rumours puts one in mind of the similar rumours that circulated in Lourdes during the month when the grotto was out of bounds (René Laurentin, *Lourdes, Documents authentiques,* Paris, Lethielleux, 1958, pp. 21-30). It is perhaps significant that those who come to pray at Grouchevo are Catholics, who are outside the law, and Orthodox, who are recognised legally. In spite of their antagonism they pray with one heart. Gifts pour in spontaneously to Grouchevo just as they did at Lourdes in 1858 (according to one report as much as 62,000 roubles). The police have confiscated the money and lodged it to a peace fund.

What can we conclude from this hazy and sometimes contradictory evidence?

1. Little Maria believed she saw the Virgin at least once and perhaps on other occasions. But not for a long period and not

continuously. What she may have said can only reach us through a filter of caution, fear and extrapolation so that it is difficult to give an accurate appraisal.

2.   After a first phase of repression even police action was reduced to passive surveillance by one militiaman and during the three summer months of 1987 three times the number of Lvov-Grouchevo tickets were sold as had been sold during the three previous years. But perhaps this liberal attitude is due to the insignificance of the imprint on an old plank which crowds come to look at. It may well be that the Party finds it reassuring; is it not further confirmation of the subjective nature of religion and a further indication of the official doctrine that religion is the opium of the masses?

A stifled faith looks for signs
In the presence of this drama of fear and faith we should not be too quick to point an accusing finger and declare illuminism. Grouchevo is Catholic but the Church is outlawed and therefore exists clandestinely. A faith which is stifled will grasp at any sign; even the tiniest icons are treasured. Prophetic rumours abound.

> One of the soldiers was ordered to shoot at the window where the Virgin appeared (according to one of the earlier witnesses). But he dropped dead on attempting to carry out the order. Then the window was blocked with opaque material. But the brightness shone through (second witness in the *Bulletin* of the Christian community).

But there is nothing to confirm any of this, not the death, the covering plank or the light shining through.

What is at stake here is not simple exaltation but rather the permanent challenge of faith under constant pressure, a faith that picks up every crumb and knows how to discover God in this void. Ultimately this is what emerges from the evidence of the two believing (and critical) witnesses already quoted above.

> We left the area of the church and were making our way to the bus stop. On the way we questioned passers-by, both men and women. When we asked one man what happened

he replied that he knew nothing about it. When we asked another if he believed in what was happening he replied: 'Around here, who does not believe?' and he showed us a house where we could get further information.

We went towards the courtyard of this house. The woman who was there had seen us approaching and she warned us to leave as quickly as possible. On the previous day, four men, either monks or a priest and his companions had been 'lifted' and forcibly put on the bus, 'so that they never even got as far as the church'. The woman was visibly afraid.

We went to the station and we waited for the bus. Just then two women and a man passed on the way to the church. They returned ten minutes later saying that they had been sent back by a militiaman. They had barely had the time to go to the back of the cloister to pray for a short time and to gather some earth. One of the women, a religious, said 'May God be praised that the militiaman was so well mannered. He allowed us to gather some earth from the spot where the Virgin had been. The main thing is that we were allowed to go there and that the angel has inscribed us in his book.'

She gave us some of this earth. We accepted it as a pardon from Our Lady for not having thought of gathering some ourselves, for not having seen the signs of her apparition and for having doubted.

From the conversion of Constantine to the conversion of Gorbachev?

So are these apparitions in Eastern Bloc countries just an illusion? No, there are some genuine cases. When I am told of these it is always under seal of the greatest secrecy; I am expressly forbidden to leak any information, not even the name of the country where they happen. The individuals or groups concerned would be exposed to too much danger. The marvels from these catacombs will be revealed one day. For that to happen the miraculous conversion of Constantine would have to be repeated in the case of Gorbachev and his friends. Constantine was an absolute emperor but Gorbachev is just the leader of the immovable state apparatus which provides constant proof of its power.

The apparitions at Fatima foretold the conversion of Russia and we remember the answer which Little R got to her question: 'Russia will not be able to resist my power and then I will make it resplendent with the light from my Immaculate Heart.' Perhaps we are witnessing a re-echoing of the message of Fatima like that heard by the visionaries of Medjugorje: 'Russia will be the country where I will be most honoured'.

Appendix 2

APPARITIONS WITHOUT CREDIBILITY

I will not dwell too long on those apparitions where there is evidence of weakness. There is no question of pillorying those who have been in error, however partially. Very often their initial experience of prayer was healthy. Lack of spiritual guidance in an area that abounds in temptations and psycho-physiological traps allowed them to deviate, to confuse their own drives with the movements of the Spirit. Where such errors are evident an apparition cannot become a model, a place of pilgrimage. Discretion becomes the order of the day. It is much better to state this clearly. Not that one wants to throw the first stone but rather one prays that these so-called visionaries will find their way back from these ambivalent experiences to a humble faith. Some have succeeded in this in a most praiseworthy fashion. In many cases they were left to their own devices because their very failure had caused them to be abandoned and left without advice of any sort. Here are some examples:

Bayside

In the state of New York, Mrs Veronica Leuken has received messages since 25 July 1975. She immediately records them on a tape recorder. But these sincere messages contain evident errors. They denounce Cardinal Villot and the future Cardinal Benelli, the Pope's two principal collaborators, as being 'men given to Satan'. They were alleged to have substituted an impostor, altered by plastic surgery, for the Pope.

In a French language colour magazine about Bayside (*Vers demain, pèlerins,* Rougemont, Canada) we read the following: 'An impostor rules in the place of Paul VI. He is a creature of the minds of Satan's agents. One of the best plastic surgeons has been employed to create this impostor.... My child, shout this from the roof-tops.'

We find the same thing in R.S. Catta, *Message de Bayside, New York, 1975-1976. Des jours d'apocalypse,* Sherbrooke, Éditions Saint-Raphaël, 1978: 'The Pope Paul VI who appears in public is not the real pope (p. 127). Everything is now ready for the surrender of the Church into the hands of the satanic synagogue which rules the Church. The Pope is really a prisoner in his rooms (p. 130). Our Lady weeps with her hands over her eyes (p. 157). (cf. René Laurentin, *Bulletin,* in *Revue des sciences philosophiques et théologiques* 60, 1976, p. 496; and 65, 1981, pp. 327-328).

Belluno, Italy

Francesca Payer, a brilliant and exuberant girl, drew crowds of pilgrims and priests to witness her sincere and fervent ecstasies. At the age of fourteen she had her first apparition in June 1985 while playing with her companions in her garden. On 2 December 1985 Dr Margnelli did some tests during her ecstasy but did not find any of the characteristics of ecstasy. Her case was widely discussed. She has returned discreetly to ordinary life. (cf Drs Marco Margnelli and G. Gagliardi, *Le Apparizioni della Madonna,* special edition of *Riza Scienze*, July 1987, no. 16, pp. 70-72 — with a picture of the supposed ecstasy on p. 71). I have received a number of video-tapes dealing with Francesca's visions and containing interviews with the girl.

Palmar de Troya (Spain)

It all began with an apparition to three children on 30 March 1968. Very soon there were enormous crowds (20,000 on 15 May 1970) and there was also an increase in the number of visionaries. On 18 May 1970 the Archbishop of Seville denounced the event as 'collective hysteria which has nothing to do with real religion'. Fr Luna in his work *La Mère de Dieu m'a souri,* Paris, Nouvelles Éditions Latines, 1973, has endeavoured to defend these apparitions, including communion given by invisible angels (colour photo of this communion on the cover of the book).

The messages, which were attributed to Our Lady, dealt with the Mass in Latin and the evolution of Spain in the post-Franco era. At the outset they said nothing of the Pope. But in December 1974 the messages began to say that the Pope was drugged by his attendants. It was in this climate that Mgr Ngo Dhin Thuc (a brother of the assassinated president of Vietnam, Diem) ordained priests (1 January 1976) and later, on 11 January, bishops. (See *Vida Nueva,* no. 1014, 24 January 1976, pp. 139-141). Though excommunicated by the Pope these bishops went ahead with further ordinations (illicit though presumed valid) of five bishops and eleven priests. (*Vida Nueva,* 7 February 1976, no. 1016, p. 231; 14 February 1976, no. 1017, p. 317; *ICI,* 1 February 1976, no. 498, pp. 30-31). There were further ordinations at the end of February. At that stage young Clemente Dominguez, who was blind, declared himself pope and named six cardinals from among the forty-three bishops he had ordained — all the able-bodied men of the community. About twenty of them (all young) came to visit Kerizinen. They all wore classical episcopal vestments. This pomp and ceremony attracted a lot of attention and resulted in numerous articles (seven of them in *Sur-Oeste,* a Seville daily and in particular two numbers of *Documentación ecclesiástica,* published by the Archbishop of Seville under the title *Los Sucesos de El. Palmar de Troya,* Seville, 1976 also *Ephemerides Mariological 27,* 1977, pp. 451-452).

L.J. Luna (*Le vrai et le faux Palmar,* 59790 Bonchamp, 400, avenue Jean-Javres et 7713 Marquain, Belgique, ed. Hovine, 1979), endeavours to save Palmar by dissociating those members who remained obedient to the Church from the schismatics: 'The real visionaries, Maria Marin, Maria Luisa Vila, Rosario Arenillos and Pepe Cajetano' continued their community life elsewhere. Today the whole affair has abated.

Pescara
Don Vincenzo, an ex-footballer, had been four years ordained and was assistant parish priest at Monte Silvano which is directly opposite the Yugoslav port of Split which in turn is about 150 kilometres from Medjugorje. In 1987 he led a group of about 700 people to Yugoslavia. He had set up a very strong prayer group. There were night vigils and sessions on Christian education and the results were admirable. He was then charged with the spiritual direction of the visionary Maria Antonina Fioritti (32). It was intended that neither her ecstasies nor the messages she received would be made public.

In his enthusiasm he did not observe the silence imposed by his bishop. The priest and the visionary held a press conference at which great signs were foretold for 28 February 1988: one was to be a sign in the sun during daylight hours, as at Fatima, and the other would be seen in the night sky towards midnight. The news was announced in outlandish terms: 'Pescara will be the conclusion of Medjugorje'; 'These will be the greatest apparitions in history.' This sensationalism contradicts the messages of Medjugorje.

Father Carlo Colona, a Jesuit and a friend of the bishop, held a rival press conference at which he denounced these disturbing predictions. The bishop himself intervened personally. Nevertheless a crowd of about 120,000 together with reporters from press and television turned up to witness the event. Nothing happened apart from the general disappointment of the huge crowd. The priest recognised the error of his ways and on the advice of his bishop he went for a long retreat to a monastery. But nobody seems to be worried about the visionary who is alone in her distress. These events demonstrate how easily fervour can degenerate into illuminism, how Satan can disguise himself as an angel of light (cf. 2 Cor 11:14), and how human frailty can whip the flames of enthusiasm into illusory and foolish predictions. We can readily understand the importance of constant vigilance, humility and discernment and the Church's reason for calling for prudence.

Little Pebble
Little Pebble, a convert from atheism, had the good sense to hide his real name and his identity in order to give more prominence to his messages. But he then undertook to travel round the world to advertise these messages. He handed out a photo of himself with the Pope (taken during a general audience) and presented a form of approval allegedly given to him by priests and visionaries at Medjugorje. They subsequently denied any knowledge of this. His bishop came out against these excesses (some of which are described on p. 45 above).

Quebec
Marie-Paule Giguère, founder of the Army of Mary. She was born on 14 September 1921 at Sainte Germaine du lac Etchemin, in Quebec. In her fifteen-volume autobiography, *Vie d'Amour,* she recounts the sorrows and joys of her life. She had founded the Army of Mary on 28 May 1971 with the objectives of prayer and sanctification. It was approved by the canonical decree of Archbishop Maurice Roy on 10 March 1975. The movement spread rapidly and many priests of the diocese informed me that it had been responsible for a renewal of prayer in their parishes. Thus, it was well-founded and had justly received recognition.

I happened to be in Quebec on 4 May 1987 when Cardinal L.A. Vachon, the Archbishop of Quebec, published a decree dissolving the Army of Mary. This followed a number of warnings against 'serious errors' which had been issued on 4 July, 15 November and 9 December 1986. Conciliation talks had broken down and Cardinal Vachon resolved to revoke the approval given in an earlier canonical decree (the documentation is published in *Documentation catholique,* 6-20 September 1987, no. 1946, pp. 864-865).

The excesses associated with illuminism are more than evident in the books of Marc Bosquart: *De la Trinité divine à l'Immaculée Trinité* and *Le Rédempteur et la Corédemptrice ,* Édition Famille des Fils et Filles de Marie, C295, Lemoilou, Quebec, Canada, 1985 and 1986.

As an example of the type of material involved, the first book attempts to establish how Marie-Paule Giguère would be the mystical reincarnation of Mary. He tries to define the consequences — his diagrams are clear but the explanations are woolly — the Immaculate Trinity which would be made up of the Spirit (a common element in the Divine Trinity and the Immaculate Trinity) Mary and Marie-Paule, a total of five persons. This gnostic superstructure is of course self-contradictory. Marie-Paule Giguère was horrified by these sentiments, as Raoul Auclair acknowledges in his preface to Marc Bosquart's book (p.17). She has now repudiated them. May the movement, which has thus compromised, become reconciled with the Archbishop of Quebec in spite of insurmountable misunderstandings.

These deviations in a movement which had initially been excellent according to a number of very serious priests, contributed in no small way to discrediting the revelations of Our Lady of all Peoples (Amsterdam 1945-59) who was on the insignia of the Army of Mary and whose picture adorned the cover of Marc Bosquart's book. A thin line divides illuminism and unbelief.

Appendix 3

CASES OF CONFLICT

ON THE WAY TO A SOLUTION THROUGH SUPPRESSION OR CAREFUL CHANNELLING

Amsterdam

Notre Dame de tous les peuples: fifty-six messages (1945-59), edited by H.A. Brouwer, *Le message de la Dame de tous les peuples*, Amsterdam, 1967, followed by additional documentation for the subsequent years up to 8 September 1973. On 29 January 1973 the Bishop of Haarlem expressed grave doubts about these apparitions. He expressed his regret at not being able to forego the renewal of the canonical prohibitions issued by the Congregation for Doctrine and Faith (letter from Cardinal Seper, 24 May 1972). He had foreseen a time when these devotions could be treated more liberally, following insistent and respectful requests from the devotees of the apparitions. But the Congregation of Doctrine and Faith, in a letter of 25 May 1974, saw no reason to change the negative judgment (René Laurentin, *Bulletin,* in *Revue des sciences philosophiques et théologiques* 58, 1974, p. 321, note 181 and 60, 1976, p. 495).

Balestrino

In the diocese of Albenga near Ventimiglia: Catherine Richero is said to have had 150 apparitions from 1949 (when she was seven years old) to 1969. A short message was given out after each apparition. According to a letter from the vicar general of Albenga, published in *L'Ami du clergé* 79, (1969, p.506) the apparitions do not imply 'either theological or moral error or any suggestion of a new devotion. But there is no indication of the supernatural'. Hence it was forbidden to go to the place of the alleged apparitions (Diocesan letters of 15 July 1950, 28 July 1954, 25 July 1955, 28 June 1957. G. Lanfray, *Pèlerinage à Balestrino* and René Laurentin, *Bulletin* in *Revue des sciences philosophiques et théologiques 54,* 1970, pp. 310-311, note 95).

Garabandal (Spain)

Apparitions to Conchita Gonzalez and to three other visionaries between 1960 and 1965. Four official statements were published by successive bishops of Santander — Doroteo Fernandez, Eugenio Beitia Aldazabal and Vicente Puchol Montis. The second of these states: 'The supernatural character is not apparent.' 'All the events that have taken place in this locality have a natural explanation', stated Mgr Puchol on 18 March 1967. This view was confirmed by Cardinal Ottaviani. The visionaries retracted. 'It was a spontaneous retraction' according to Mgr Puchol in a letter to me written a few days before he was killed in a car accident in May 1967. In an interview in 1971 Conchita admitted that on 15 August 1967 'I was going to tell a priest that I had never seen the Virgin, that I wanted to tell the bishop that it was an illusion or a dream or even a lie. Afterwards at Pampleune ... I said to the bishop that I had never seen the Virgin and that I had been deceiving everyone all along .... These doubts lasted five or six days. Since that time I have been confused and have doubts and I am now waiting for a miracle to prove whether it is true or false' (Harry Daley, *Miracle at Garabandal,* Dublin, Ward River Press, 1985, p. 189).

Nevertheless there are still fervent devotees of Garabandal. Many books have been published by the likes of Frs Combes and Lafineur, Robert Francis Turner, OP, and the late J.A. Pelletier as well as by E. Sanchez Ventura y Pascual (who was converted at Garabandal). There are even audio tapes and a film. The *Magazine of Garabandal* has appeared in America (No. 1: January 1978, PO Box 606, Lindenhurst, New York, NY 11757).

The affair is very complex. One might question the enthusiasm which surrounded the visionaries and may have facilitated the proliferation of wonders. What is the importance of the retraction made by the visionaries? I questioned Conchita about this in New York in mid-July 1986. It was at the end of a prayer meeting which is held in her house every week. She did not give me any answers. This was perhaps wise on her part. She is now concentrating on rearing her four children. A weekly rosary is held in her house and attracts a large number of people. The act of reparation to the Sacred Heart, forgotten since the Council, is read though there is no mention of Garabandal.

The present bishop, J.A. del Val Gallo, had thought of finding a peaceful pastoral solution. But the devotees of Garabandal broke this news too quickly. Rome then urged the maintenance of the status quo, no doubt the result of the indiscretion of the devotees.

In spite of many shocks and disappointments the visionaries have made excellent progress but the extraordinary events of 1961 to 1965 still defy explanation: 'Communion from the hands of invisible angels', ecstasies involving deformation of the neck (as happens in the case of hysterics though the lives of the visionaries show no evidence that they were in fact hysterics), spectacular falls, etc. On the negative side there is a lack of transparency and the prediction of marvels which never actually happened. According to the devotees of Garabandal the great sign has been held back because of opposition. According to some this was why the apparitions at Medjugorje took place.

The present bishop has succeeded in calming the situation. He has met Conchita and was able to see for himself the excellent progress she has made. Pilgrimages have almost disappeared at Garabandal. Individual pilgrims are welcome on the parish premises where, of course, there is no talk of apparitions.

On the considerable bibliography which exists on Garabandal see my *Bulletins* in *Revue des sciences philosophiques et théologiques,* 52 (1968), pp. 528-529, note 159: episcopal documents; 54 (1970) p. 311, note 95, which refers to the closely written documentation by J.M. Alonso in *Ephemerides mariologicae,* 19 (1969), pp. 475-488; 56 (1972), p. 468, note 95; 58 (1974), p. 320, note 179; 60 (1976), p. 495, note 224; 62 (1978), p. 297, note 154; 65 (1981), p. 326, note 120.

The limits of the enthusiastic apologists for Garabandal are underlined by Dom B. Billet, *Note sur Garabandal, Esprit et Vie,* 4 December 1980, pp. 625-626: cf. *Cahiers marials* (1 April 1971), No. 77, pp. 122-123.

Among the most serious studies are those of Fr F. Turner OP, *Tout le peuple l'écoutait, suspendu à ses lèvres,* 68380 Chazay d'Azergues, ed. A. Combes, 1975: a brief account of the events and a study of the principal themes; *Moi, votre Mère, je vous aime. Ainsi parlait Marie à Garabandal,* Paris, Editions Pierre Téqui, 1980, which is an update of a previous book; J. Warszawski, *El mito de Garabandal,* Madrid, Studium, 1973: a serious and moderate plea for the authenticity of Garabandal which appeared under a *nihil obstat* from the vicariate of Rome; *Congrès mondial d'études sur Garabandal,* Lourdes, 18-20 August 1978, Chazay d'Azergues, ed. A. Combes, 1980, gathers evidence from many witnesses, both priests and doctors. The witness of E. Sanchez Ventura Y Pascual, *La vierge, apparaît-elle à Garabandal?,* Paris, NEL, 1965, are both moving and sincere.

San Damiano

Rosa Quattrini (1909-81) gave birth to two children by caesarian section in 1938 and 1943. She refused to follow her doctors' advice when they wanted her to have a 'therapeutic' abortion on becoming pregnant with a third child. 'It is God who has given me this child', she said. The birth was nevertheless a success but Rosa's health suffered and she was subsequently confined to bed both at home and in hospital for long periods. She was unexpectedly cured on 29 September 1961 by a mysterious visit. The apparitions of Our Lady began on 16 October 1964. From then on the apparitions took place every week. There was a message which Rosa herself disseminated. On the orders of the bishop she allowed others to spread the message from 1968 onwards and in 1970 all dissemination of the messages was forbidden. Mama Rosa claimed to have received from Our Lady a project for a 'city of roses'. She received spontaneous gifts for this purpose but this led to accusations of fraud; similar accusations are levelled against priests in the Eastern Bloc where money which is not earned is considered to have been acquired by fraud. At her death she bequeathed everything to Pope John Paul II. He refused the bequest on the advice of the Bishop of Piacenza, Mgr Enrico Manfredini. This bishop was later promoted to the cardinalate and the See of Bologna (though his sudden death prevented him from taking up this office). His successor would seem to have been given the task of easing the tension between the many pilgrims and the bishop's palace. A void existed particularly in relation to the liturgy. There was no longer any priest at San Damiano. A priest has now been appointed who celebrates daily Mass and welcomes pilgrims while maintaining a strictly reserved position with regard to the apparitions. The pilgrims have appreciated the improvement in the situation and they attend this Mass with great discretion and in a spirit of obedience. Mama Rosa had been left too much on her own and she became the victim of traditionalist priests who began to influence her messages to the detriment of her own reputation (see above, pp. 26-27).

For a bibliography on this question: René Laurentin, *Bulletins* in *Revue des sciences philosophiques et théologiques:* 60 (1976), p. 495, note 226; 62 (1978), p. 297, note 253; 65 (1981), p. 325-326, note 119, and in particular 70 (1986), pp. 139-140 where there is a review of one of the best documented books on the question: Roland Maisonneuve and Michel de Belsunce, *San Damiano: Histoire et documents,* Paris, Téqui, 1983, 384 pp.

In France there have been two apparitions which have received negative judgments from the bishops.

Kérizinen (Finistère)

Jeanne Louise Ramonet, born in 1910, is said to have had visions of 'The Virgin of the Rosary', sometimes accompanied by the Sacred Heart, on seventy-one occasions between 15 September 1938 and 1 October 1965. On 9 December 1949, she was asked to have a church built. A spring appeared on 13 July 1950 and it is alleged that the sun danced four times between 1953 and 1954. The message encourages the recitation of the rosary, the struggle against the devil, the proclamation of the salvation of the world through the sorrowing heart of Mary and the inauguration of the reign of the merciful heart of Jesus. Communiqués from the Bishop of Quimper forbade people to go to the sanctuary which had been built in spite of his prohibition: (*Ami du clergé* 78, 1968, p. 601; René Laurentin, *Bulletin* in *Revue des sciences philosophiques et théologiques,* 54 (1970), p. 311 56 (1972), p. 468, note 95; 58 (1974), p. 321, note 180: a new warning by Mgr Francis Barbu, on 20 May 1972; 60 (1976), p. 495, no. 225: approval of the Bishop of Quimper by the Congregation of the Faith (on 21 June 1975) for the 'wise and prudent' proposals he put to that office on 27 February. The bishop subsequently opposed a proposal, launched in May 1975, to build a new chapel of 1200m^2. (*Documentation catholique,* 7-21 September 1975, no. 1682, pp. 779-782). The negative judgment on the supernatural character of the events does not seem to impugn the good character of the visionary who is a pious and discreet lady.

The same occurs with the negative judgment on Dozulé, where there have been apparitions of Christ. These do not enter into the subject matter of this book. As in Kérizinen the visionary, who in this instance is a catechist for her parish, is beyond reproach. She has reservations about the publication of her message by Éditions Résiac, 1984 (*La croix glorieuse de Dozulé*) but accepts that published by Éditions NEL.

Penablanca (Chile)

Michel Angel Poblet was born on 27 May 1966. He was abandoned by his mother after eight days and subsequently cared for by another woman. Because she could no longer afford to keep him she transferred him to an orphanage when he was nine years old. He claims to have seen the Virgin on the hill of Penablanca since 12 June 1983. Fr Contado, a Jesuit, is his spiritual mentor.

His message concerns conversion and salvation for lost souls, the holiness of priests, devotion to the rosary, to the Blessed Sacrament, to the Passion of Christ and the imminence of a catastrophe for humanity.

He received the stigmata. He was also given communion by the Archangel Michael. Mgr F. de Borja Valenzuela Rios has adopted a negative stance: 'I am inclined towards a strongly critical (negative) attitude of this affair and I forbid priests to celebrate any cult in this place' (6 October 1983). The text, laid out in five points, does not give any reasons and it is, therefore, difficult to form a clear view. It has been said that some of the messages were favourable to the Pinochet regime and this would have damaged the apparitions enormously. But this rumour and the many accusations levelled against the visionary by the press (all of which he denies) do not make for easy clarification.

Appendix 4

APPARITIONS AT ÎLE BOUCHARD
(8-14 DECEMBER 1947)

It was on 8 December, the feast of the Immaculate Conception, that the apparitions at Île Bouchard began in the parish church. Île Bouchard is a village situated between the two branches of the Loire in the diocese of Tours.

Twelve-year-old Jacqueline Aubry, her sister Jeannette (seven), their cousin Nicole Robin (ten) and Laura Croizon (eight) saw Our Lady and received this message: 'Tell the little children to pray for France, because she is in great need'.

Historians of Île Bouchard are struck by the coincidence between these apparitions and the troubled situation in France which was being threatened by a communist take-over. There were very serious tensions — strikes, deaths, 106 convictions for sabotage at the beginning of December and the mysterious death and subsequent funeral of Marshall Leclerc (Monday 8 December). It was during the night of 8-9 December that Benoît Frachon was able to arrange a return to work and to calm.

The apparitions lasted for a week from Monday 8 December to the following Sunday. They are clear. Signs were given, one of which was an inexplicable ray of sunlight which shone on visionaries during the final apparition and this in a church into which the sun cannot penetrate.

Jacqueline and her sister came from a non-practising family: 'Only my grandmother attended Sunday Mass. At home there was never any mention of God or the Blessed Virgin.'

The apparitions have not been the object of a negative judgment nor has any disapproval been expressed. They have simply been surrounded by silence and restriction. Perhaps the real reason for this is the fact that the eldest of the visionaries had for a number of years been subjected to brutal maltreatment on the part of a certain group, involving drugs etc. Nobody came to her aid until a commandant of the gendarmerie, head of the crime squad, was alerted by a military chaplain who came to Tours to put an end to these abuses. Everybody wanted discretion and so the affair was brought to an end simply by threatening the culprits; no charge was ever levelled against them. This discretion was no doubt welcomed by the anti-clerics and even the clergy, who were to some degree involved, and perhaps even by the victim herself. It is nevertheless regrettable that this conspiracy of silence has cast a shadow over the apparitions ever since. How did the visionary put up with this abuse which ruined her health, without changing her spiritual life? The answer is her total abandonment to God and to Mary with whom she remains in constant contact. Jacqueline has a mysterious vocation to suffer. She no longer shows this on the outside but she continues to live it in a different and more interior way. She is faithful to this vocation. I am astonished at the work God is doing within her and at the quiet patience with which she accepts this in the Lord.

The annual pilgrimage on 8 December continues every year. More and more people come but in a discreet fashion. On the occasion of the anniversary Mass on 8 December there was no mention of the apparitions. The prayerful presence of one of her former persecutors at the celebrations to mark the fortieth anniversary was ample proof that Jacqueline had not suffered in vain.

Appendix 5

MARY'S MESSAGES TO DON GOBBI, FOUNDER OF THE MARIAN PRIESTLY MOVEMENT

Since 7 July 1973, Don S. Gobbi, a fifty-year-old Italian priest has been transmitting messages from Our Lady to the Marian Priestly Movement which he founded.

The first views I sought on this movement, those of Cardinal Pellegrino, the theologian S. de Fiores and a number of other mariologists, were reserved, even severe. They criticised the abundance and the sentimentalism of the messages. I myself was perplexed by the situation particularly when comparing the extraordinary number of editions of the messages (which are published in all languages) with the number of priests involved. For many years I had never met a member of the Marian Priestly Movement even at the mariological societies which I attended.

During my travels I have met some members in various countries. There would appear to be about 100 in France, 1,000 in America and thousands all over the world, though the figure of 60,000 priests and tens of millions of lay members does seem exaggerated (twelfth edition of the collection of messages, *La Vierge à ses fils de prédilection: les prêtres,* Milan, 1986. p.45). Those whom I have met are very serious, down-to-earth priests who respond to the needs of their people. What they require from the movement is a stimulus which does not take over either their lives or their preaching. The relative success of the movement, in spite of the fact that it has all the ingredients which attract the scorn of the intelligentsia, shows that in the people of God there is need not only for a solid interior life of sacrifice and generosity but also for a more direct means of communication, for signs. This is true of both priests and people. There is much talk of pluralism. But why are we so indulgent towards the various manifestations of the secular and so critical of heavenly fervour and signs? When we examine things closely this critical attitude is not always justified.

Personally, I have never felt the need for apparitions. Instinctively I look for my spiritual nourishment elsewhere and not in the fervent messages received by Don Gobbi. I am not necessarily proud of this attitude and it is perhaps true that my faith is lacking in warmth or enthusiasm as a result. I believe that the movement is worthy of respect even though this also has its risks. At a time when many clergy are in fact leaving the ministry this movement has been of great benefit to many priests whom I have met. As regards Don Gobbi, I was surprised at his appearance. I had expected to find a bubbly character but instead he was a rather fat, balding fifty-year-old who spoke with calm deliberation. One would certainly not expect the abundance and the sentimentality of the messages to originate from such a man. After fifteen years these messages form a volume of 798 pages. (*La Vierge à ses fils de prédilection: les prêtres,* p. 150).

The Pope and the Holy See, mindful of the fruits which this movement has borne, have encouraged Don Gobbi. Yet he has not received official approval. The change of spiritual director (15 April 1985) has not altered Don Gobbi's position. He continues to lead and guide the movement.

A number of the messages are of an apocalyptic nature, in particular the message of 3 July 1987:

> This year the era of your heavenly mother will begin strikingly and officially. It is a time when my appeal to you is most urgent: return, return, O lost and perverted humanity. Return to the paths of conversion, return to your Lord and Saviour. This is the time of the great return.... The time allotted to you for your conversion has almost passed. The days are counted ... the cup of divine anger is full, it is full to overflowing.
>
> Iniquity covers the entire earth. The Church is overshadowed by apostasy and sin. The Lord, overcome by mercy, will proceed to purify you by the powerful action of his justice and love. Even greater sorrows and greater tragedies lie in store for you. These latter times are nearer than you might think. Already this year, some of the great events which I predicted at Fatima will come true. I have told this as a secret to the young people of Medjugorje to whom I appear....
>
> After the period of great suffering will come the period of renewal and humanity will once again be a garden of living beauty.... You will see the new earth and the new heavens.

The Father ardently desires to pour out torrents of divine love on a suffering humanity ....

1987 has come and gone and we have not seen the fulfilment of any of the great events predicted at Fatima or Medjugorje. Thus the revelation of the ten secrets which was awaited by many has not in fact taken place. But there is nothing extraordinary about that. I had already warned those who spoke to me about this expectation: even the most authentic predictions — those which took place in the primitive Christian community at the time of St Paul — had a tendency to run events into each other and to bring them forward.

The essence of the message is God's and Mary's tenderness for priests, his favourite sons. It is an invitation to prayer and to generosity but also to sacrifice and suffering and, of course, to chastity, according to the message given on 11 February 1977, the feast day of Our Lady of Lourdes.

> I want you to be pure in spirit, pure in mind and in body.... In these modern times this has become more difficult for you because of the errors which abound and which tend to depreciate the value of your real consecration. How many priests, my beloved sons, have given up their priesthood because the Holy Father wants to retain celibacy! But there are many others who do not leave the ministry and who do not observe this law, either because they believe it to be old-fashioned or on the way out or even because within themselves they feel that celibacy is unjustified and they are therefore no longer bound by it ....
>
> Today many of my priests live in impurity. O my beloved sons! Relive again in your bodies the virginity of my Son Jesus and the stigmata of his passion. Your priestly body ought to be a crucified body: crucified by the world and its seductions (*La Vierge à ses fils de prédilection: les prêtres,* twelfth edition, 1986, pp. 274-277).

For fifty years, the Church had maintained a silence on the subject of new apparitions, speaking only to point out those which had been the object of a negative judgement. Yet now there is much more open discussion. Why is this?

It has largely to do with the abolition of Canon 1385 of the old *Code of Canon Law* which banned all books and publications describing new apparitions, revelations, visions, prophecies and miracles, or proposing new devotions, even under the pretext that they are private.

It was Paul VI who abolished this Canon, five years after the close of the Council, on 14 October 1970 (Decree of the Congregation for the Doctrine of the Faith, *Acta Apostolicae Sedis*, 29 December 1970, p. 1186). This article was therefore omitted from the new *Code of Canon Law*. Apparitions were no longer to be kept in the dark.

This new liberalisation is in accordance with the Christian liberty which the Council restored to favour, placing greater confidence in the graces and the prophetic initiatives of the laity. Yet it can only prove itself and endure if Christians use it with discernment, moderation and obedience to their bishops, who must watch over these phenomena, which are not free from risks, with the same authority and prudence as they formerly exercised.

My wish is that this book may help towards a responsible judgement.

Appendix 6

NEW APPARITIONS/NEW INFORMATION

South Africa
At Gomé in Zululand, 180km north of Durban, presumed apparitions of the Virgin to Sr Reinolda May, OSB.

Ten apparitions took place between 2 August 1955 and 2 May 1971. The Virgin asked to be invoked by the title 'Tabernacle of the Most High' (a title vouched for by the Greek Fathers), and requested that a chapel be built. In 1976 a commission of inquiry judged that there was insufficient reason to accept these facts (avoiding any condemnation). People still continue to come and pray at Gomé, at the place of the 'seven springs'. (Seven is a symbolic figure — there are actually many more than that, and the visitors draw water from them.) This perseverance in prayer continues to question the Church, with the enlightened support of the Gomé Shrine Committee, in collaboration with the fifty-six-year-old Bishop of Leshouve, Mgr Mansuet Byase, who has been gripped once again by the question, at the time of writing. The traditional character and the fruits of the piety at this shrine could lead to its pastoral acceptance and to *de facto* recognition of the cult, if not to official recognition depending on circumstances of which the Bishop is the best judge.

England
Presumed apparitions to Patricia (whose surname is omitted to protect her anonymity), a mother of three living in the suburbs of south-west London. She sees Christ and the Virgin and receives messages concerned principally with opposing the abortion of 'crucified innocence', since 19 February 1985. These messages have been published in English and French in a forty-page booklet called *Je suis la splendide Étoile du matin qui se lève avec le nouvel age de l'innocence divine: message donné par Jesus et Marie à Patricia en Angleterre*, published by Les amis de l'innocence divine triomphante, le Gonnec, BP 69, 83510 Lorgues, France.

Burundi
In this country which is afflicted by racist massacres, numerous apparitions have been reported, none of which show appear to

be serious. Agitation, contagion and even simulation are the apparent causes.

Cameroon

Since 13 May 1986, in the mother house of the Daughters of Mary (native sisters) at Nsimalen, eight schoolchildren claim to have seen the Virgin. Jacqueline Atargana, a six-year-old who had been deaf and dumb since birth, was claimed to be the first visionary. She spoke for the first time, crying 'Mary! Mary! Mary!' and pointing at the apparitions. Pierre Zang Nvondo, a forty-one-year-old catechist reports that he recovered his sight beneath the tree where the Virgin appears. Mgr Zoa, Bishop of Yaounde, advises prudence and reserve, in anticipation of a study according to the criteria of the Church.

Costa Rica

A book entitled *El cielo no avisa* has been published, telling of heavenly messages in that country. As yet, I have been unable to obtain a copy. It tells of messages without apparitions.

France, Paris

Le Monde of 11 September, *La Croix* of 13 September and several other newspapers mentioned 'apparitions of the Virgin' to Bassan Assaf, servant of Michel Merhey, a wealthy Syrian living in a luxurious residence on rue Octave-feuillet in the sixteenth arrondissement, Paris. His skin began to exude oil on 12 August 1988. Cures were attributed to this oil. Gerard Majax, the illusionist, came to monitor the visionary but no oil appeared. A similar phenomenon was noted at Damascus in the case of Myrna (see pp. 72-82). The events in Paris appear to be sincere and are recognised by the Church, yet their context and the publicity accorded them indicate a need for great caution.

Haiti

A private apparition of the Virgin to one of the three sisters in the little community founded by Mgr Ligonde, Archbishop of Port-au-Prince. Awaiting a sign from the Virgin, they asked him to celebrate Mass for them on 25 March 1987. During this Mass, thirteen beggars coming from thirteen different parishes arrived at the house claiming that a lady dressed in blue told them, 'Today is a feast day. You will find something to eat here this evening.'

Ireland
In a grotto at Melleray, from 16 to 24 August 1985, Ursula O'Rourke (17) Tom Cliffe (12) and Barry Budley (11) received apparitions of the Virgin and messages to humanity. 'Humanity has ten years in which to convert and pray' or grave consequences would result. The bishop is conducting an open-minded examination of the question. (W. Davy, *Notre Dame apparait en Irlande: Melleray*, Hauteville (Switzerland) Editions du Parvis, 1988).

Italy
Caslano (near the Swiss border)
Guiseppe Casagrande (nicknamed Pino) was born on 22 July 1924, married in 1950, and had two daughters. In 1983 he was living at Caslano, in Ticino. On 13 August of that year, he felt urged to photograph a monstrance with his polaroid. He was amazed to see the face of Jesus on his photograph. Since then he has taken about a hundred photos like this and submitted them to experts who have discounted any possibility of faking. On 9 August 1986, while praying with friends, Pino had his first apparition of the Virgin. Since then he sees her regularly in various places along the Swiss-Italian border, according to a regular programme set by the apparition. Doctor Gagliardi has testified in my presence to his ecstasies and his insensitivity to pain. Pino received ten secrets concerning menaces to the world. The apparitions have had a profound effect on his life; he now attends daily Mass etc. He and his wife share an authentic and balanced fervour. The bishop has reservations on the question of the apparitions.

I am snowed under with accounts of all the other apparitions in Italy (Patrizia Bortolotti and Piero Mantero, *Guida alle apparizioni mariane in Italia*, Milan, Edizioni Sugar, 1988, 272p.), especially:

Borello di Belpasso
Apparitions to Rosario Toscano since 4 May 1986 (pp. 217-246), judged genuine by Don G. Amorth in *Madre di Dio*, November 1988, p. 29.

Belluno
Apart from the apparitions of Francesca Pajer, there are those of Giovanni del Farra since 18 December 1985 (pp. 125-156).

Carpi
Apparitions to Gianni Varini, upon which the bishop has passed a negative judgment.

Casavatore
Since 8 December 1985, some girls from the secondary school see the Virgin in a tree and receive a message of prayer. The communist Mayor, Antonio Seller, who initially opposed them now sees the apparitions also (pp. 261-262).

Gargallo di Campi
Apparitions to a little girl since 7 July 1984, and to Giancarlo Varini since 3 December 1984. A message of love, and on 31 May 1986, the announcement of an atomic accident after Chernobyl (pp. 157-173).

Modena
Gianni Varini And some others (pp. 247-265).

Lithuania
Some newspapers here carried articles on apparitions which allegedly began in 1939. However it is very difficult to be in any way precise about the Eastern Bloc countries. (See the account of Grouchevo, Appendix 1, pp. 133-138.)

Nigeria
Felix Emeka Onah, who signs *Servus Mariae*, claims to have had apparitions of Mary and messages since 1985 at Ede Challa, which he calls the Marian Village. Mgr Emu Eneja, Bishop of Enugu (Biafra) does not approve of these apparitions. The messages are shortly to be published in French by Éditions de l'Œil.

Peru
Since January 1988 at Cachiche, in the diocese of Ica, tears have flowed from the statue of Our Lady of Lourdes at the orphanage. Crowds have visited the statue and processions have been held.

Cachiche is ten kilometres from Ica, in the shanty-town zone surrounding the city.

Philippines
On 2 February, the Virgin is alleged to have appeared to Sr Nona Aguirre and to several women at Quezon, a suburb of Manila. Solar phenomena were witnessed and apocalyptic messages received — 'a great storm of blood'. Cardinal Sin has issued a warning and assigned a priest to study the event.

Poland
Olawa, near Wroclav
In June 1983 Kazimierz Domanski, a painter who was awaiting surgery for cerebral haemorrhage with partial paralysis, claimed to have been cured and to have received the following message:

I have cured you. You must cure others. He received the following requests:

> May a chapel be built here, that the pilgrims of the whole world may come here to pray for peace in the world. If this wish is fulfilled, great graces will result, if not there will be chastisement.... Let the rosary be prayed often (...). May people go frequently to confession ... and may they receive communion with dignity, on their knees.

The apparition allegedly approved of Don Gobbi and warned against the neo-catechumenal movement. The apparition deplored the disaffection of Australia, and of several countries of the West, notably France and Germany: 'Let these countries convert.' Cardinal Glemp seems to have had serious reservations, because the 'message' of 19 March 1988 told the visionary: 'Do not bear a grudge against the Cardinal. Pray for him. He objects that you are epileptic. He should believe in your cure and summon a medical commission' etc.

Switzerland
Vassula Ryden, born in Egypt of Greek parents on 18 June 1942, was an Orthodox Christian married to a civil servant. After a dazzling but indifferent life spent travelling the world, she was transformed by the visits and messages of an angel (in late November 1985) and then of Christ (in February 1986). She

receives the messages through hand movements and aurally. She has lived in Switzerland since August 1987.

USA
This country, which seemed to resist apparitions, now sees them increasing in number, generally in an orderly and discreet fashion.

Cankton, Louisiana
The visionary Genevieve Mary Huckady, who has been married to Comeaux since 11 November 1958, promotes a knotted rosary in which each bead is a knot. However Mgr Gerard L. Frey, Bishop of La Fayette, has asked her to cease this propaganda. It shows no evidence of the supernatural.

Cleveland
M.H., a forty-seven-year-old mother of four who wishes to remain anonymous, has received messages requesting that Our Lady 'Protector of the Faith' should be invoked. The episcopate has reservations, but the visionary has a following of serious and convinced priests. I met them at Dayton in late July 1988. The group keeps in contact with the auxiliary bishop of the diocese and their propaganda is discreet. Their co-ordinator, Richard L. Devvitt, is at 2394 Mastick Road North, Olsted, Ohio 44070.

Grosby, Texas
Apparitions which allegedly began in December 1988 seem to have little credibility.

Haverville, New Hampshire
In Haverville, *The Trumpeter* receives overabundant messages, but no visions.

Lubbock, Texas
The media has dubbed these apparitions 'the American Medjugorje'. In November 1987 Mgr Joseph W. Jaimes, parish priest of Saint John Newmann parish in Lubbock, Texas, returned from a three-month sabbatical during which he had made a pilgrimage to Medjugorje. During this first pilgrimage he fasted on bread and water for ten days and was completely cured of his hypoglycaemia. In January 1988 he made a second pilgrimage

with his parishioners. On their return, during the night of 1 March 1988, one of the parishioners, Mary Constancia, received a message which she attributed to the Virgin: 'May my Son fill you with a spirit which will transform your life and make you free …. He waits only for your prayer and for the gift of your heart.' Two weeks later she received another message. Two other parishioners who came faithfully every Monday to recite the rosary, thirty-three-year-old Theresa Verner and thirty-eight-year-old Mike Slate, a retired Air Corps officer, began to receive messages.

In the spring, these messages asked for the recitation of the entire rosary, and that it should be preceded by a celebration of the Eucharist. The number of participants grew from eighty to 1,500 people. It became necessary to relay the celebration by video to those outside the church. It was announced that there would be a sign on 15 August. A huge crowd of 12,000 people began to gather that morning and throughout the day. Most of those present, though not all, claim to have seen signs in the sun at 6.10 p.m. and there are some inconsistencies between the various accounts. The 'miraculous collection' taken up that day was divided between family services (50%), Mother Teresa (10%), Mother Angelica and her television network (10%) and Pope John Paul II (10%). The message is on the theme of most apparitions — an urgent invitation to prayer, fasting, conversion and the sacraments. Among the numerous articles on the subject, I recommend the double-page account from *L'Informateur* (Quebec, 9-22 October, pp. 10-11).

Mgr Michael J. Sheehan, Bishop of Lubbock, observes these events with caution: 'I do not discourage anybody, but neither do I encourage anybody to participate at these events.'

Santa Fe, New Mexico
Vange Gonzales, a twenty-nine-year-old mother of one child, has experienced apparitions promoting family unity. The apparition encourages the recitation of the rosary and fasting on bread and water. The first apparition took place on 25 August 1986. On 1 October a group of 200 people began to come regularly every day to the Church of Christ the King. From 8 October to the end of December there was a period of confusion when the apparitions ceased, and a short period of disillusion. A more

restrained group now meets daily to pray. The bishop has assigned two priests to follow the events.

Zaire

In 1983 the community of Sons and Daughters of Mary, Mother of Chastity (known as Mariechaste, with an address at the Mayoralty of Bandalungwa, 8 rue Maspero) began to receive messages in the Lingala language, which is the most widespread language of the region. The messages requested conversion, prayer, charity, peace and reconciliation. Cardinal Malula formed a theological and medical commission to study these facts, which have provoked numerous conversions.

I simply give this information which has reached me, without examining it in depth. I have qualified each account according to my information.

These new communiqués confirm the opinion of this book: in a less judgemental climate, it is easier to cultivate prayer as a dialogue with God. The faithful are more receptive and more open to these normal supernatural phenomena, witnessed to by the Bible and Church history, which inner messages and apparitions are. These exceptional phenomena, which had taken on the proportions of events of the greatest grandeur at a time when prophecy was relatively smothered in the Church, become local, private phenomena, most of which would not necessitate building a sanctuary of international, national, or even regional importance.

This liberalisation with regard to apparitions answers certain needs of the Christian people, who had been undernourished. The new situation can be beneficial if those who enjoy these charisms receive them with prudence, humility and discretion, within the guidance of the Church, and if priests and bishops welcome these phenomena with informed (enlightened) pastoral guidance which channels these stimulating graces towards a renewal of what is essential — liturgy and charity. This has been the case at Medjugorje and in a number of the apparitions (or messages) mentioned in this book. This seems to be a more fruitful path to follow than that of repression and of abandoning the visionaries to their own devices, which has frequently tended to induce deviations and even revolts.